PHONE CLONES

PHONE CLONES

Authenticity Work in India's Transnational Service Economy

Kiran Mirchandani

ILR Press
an imprint of
Cornell University Press
Ithaca and London

Foundation Books

Delhi • Bengaluru • Mumbai • Kolkata • Chennai • Hyderabad
Pune • Thiruvananthapuram

Published by
Cambridge University Press India Pvt. Ltd.
under the imprint of Foundation Books
Cambridge House, 4381/4 Ansari Road, Daryaganj, **New Delhi** 110 002

Cambridge University Press India Pvt. Ltd.
C-22, C-Block, Brigade M.M., K.R. Road, Jayanagar, **Bengaluru** 560 070
Plot No. 80, Service Industries, Shirvane, Sector-1, Nerul, **Navi Mumbai** 400 706
10 Raja Subodh Mullick Square, 2nd Floor, **Kolkata** 700 013
21/1 (New No. 49), 1st Floor, Model School Road, Thousand Lights, **Chennai** 600 006
House No. 3-5-874/6/4, (Near Apollo Hospital), Hyderguda, **Hyderabad** 500 029
Agarwal Pride, 'A' Wing, 1308 Kasba Peth, Near Surya Hospital, **Pune** 411 011
T.C. 25/ 2731 Lukes Lane, Ambujavilasam Road, **Thiruvananthapuram** 695 001

This edition has been published by Cambridge University Press India Pvt. Ltd. by arrangement with Cornell University Press.

First South Asia Edition 2013

ISBN 978-93-82264-86-6

Published by Manas Saikia for Cambridge University Press India Pvt. Ltd.
Printed at Bhavish Graphics, Chennai

To the inspirational lives of my grandparents
Satrupi (Mira) Kripalani
1913–2009
and
Jethanand Karamchand Makhijani
1907–2003

Contents

Acknowledgments

What started out as a small study funded by the Shastri-Indo Canadian Institute in 2001 developed into a decade-long exploration with many participants who form the bedrock of this book. I am fortunate to be located at the University of Toronto, where I received the generous support of the Social Sciences and Humanities Research Council of Canada and the opportunity to interact daily with an engaged community of feminist scholars and friends. Almost every summer, I traveled to India to meet customer service workers who generously shared their time, stories, and perspectives. I came away from each interview with a sense of awe and admiration for the women and men who work in this industry. Over the years, I shared many of their stories with my colleagues and friends. The ideas in this book developed out of conversations in meetings and classes, through email, on the telephone, over meals, and in the midst of small children. I am fortunate to have been part of such a rich transnational network, which includes Anke Allspach, Arti Dhand, Enakshi Dua, Yasmin Gopal, Nancy Jackson, Shahrzad Mojab, Sanjukta Mukherjee, Shehzad Nadeem,

Roxana Ng, Shoshana Pollock, Pushkala Prasad, Anshuman Prasad, Jack Quarter, Ashwini Tambe, Shruti Tambe, Peta Tancred, Virginia Thomas, Alissa Trotz, Shankar Vedantam, and Leah Vosko. Several graduate students helped with literature reviews and interviews. I benefited from the contributions of Srabani Maitra and Jasjit Sangha during the initial stages of this work, and Pooja Aggarwal and Hewton Ricarter Moreira Tavares in latter years. Frances Benson, Candace Akins, Susan C. Barnett and their team at ILR/Cornell University Press have been a pleasure to work with at every stage. My friends in Singapore, Noraini Bakri, Sharon Couteau, Sonali Desai, Anjna Kirpalani, Gaurav Kripalani, Gina Leong, and Lo Yen Nee, nurtured my early interest in social phenomena. My brother and his family—Sandeep, Jingjing, Kai, and Ria—arranged revitalizing escapes. My wonderful family—Ashwin, Suvan, Syona, and Chipko—have given me endless joy. I thank them for being such adventurous and supportive travelers. My growing children are an enduring reminder of how long it takes to write a book and how quickly time goes by. I owe both the initiation and the successful completion of this book to my parents, Ajit and Sheeley Mirchandani, without whom none of this would have been possible. They not only provided a place from which I could do my research but also enthusiastically rearranged their entire lives for months each year to fulfill the numerous and multifaceted demands of my young family. Our time together has been the most pleasurable by-product of this project.

Abbreviations

Agent	frontline customer service worker taking calls
AHT	average handling time
BPO	business process outsourcing
C-Sat	a performance score given by customers
D-Sat	a performance score given by a dissatisfied customer
IT	information technology
ITES	information technology enabled services
MTI	Mother Tongue Influence
NASSCOM	National Association of Software and Services Companies
OJT	on-the-job training
Process	the type of work agents are engaged in (for example, processing insurance claims, solving computer problems, placing catalogue sales orders, addressing concerns with Internet connections, processing airline reservations, and so forth)
INR	rupees, the currency in India

Phone Clones

Introduction

The Authentic Clone

What happens when you need to be yourself and like someone else at the same time? This is the central demand placed on transnational service workers, who form a large and growing part of the global economy. In response, workers perform an elaborate set of largely invisible activities, which I term *authenticity work*. Based on interviews with one hundred transnational call center workers in India this book describes their authenticity work as they refashion themselves into ideal Indian workers who can expertly provide synchronous, voice-to-voice customer service for clients in the West. The experiences of Indian call center workers sheds light on a wide range of service-related activities that cross national borders. Filipino nannies refashion themselves to clone faraway employers' visions of ideal caregivers. Health workers in Mexico servicing American medical tourists strive to package the quality of their services in terms of Western professional practice. The exchange of labor and capital occurs in the context of national histories and power inequities that make the negotiation of authenticity a central part of transnational service work.

While the globalization of service work has steadily increased in recent years, there has been a dramatic shift in the nature of customer service in particular. No longer involving face-to-face interactions between customers and workers, telecommunications technologies facilitate the widespread provision of customer service that is temporally synchronous and spatially distant. Workers housed in cubicled call centers make voice-to-voice contact with customers, some of whom might live within walking distance while others are on the other side of the world. The global patterns in the offshoring of customer service work are structured not only by market forces but also by national histories. Significantly, workers living in countries that have been colonized are top contenders for offshored customer service jobs. Out of these countries, India has received the prized distinction of being the most desirable location for offshore service work.[1] Although other countries such as the Philippines, South Korea, and China have emerged as new hot spots for transnational customer service work,[2] the sector continues to grow rapidly in India, increasing by 14 percent in the 2011 financial year alone.[3] In total, the information technology and information technology enabled services (IT/ITES) sector now employs 2.5 million people in India, with service rather than software jobs as its fastest-growing segment.[4] Total revenue from the sector has grown from five billion U.S. dollars in 1997 to seventy-two billion in 2009.[5]

While the transnationalization of customer service work is relatively new, the mobility of capital without the mobility of labor has been the hallmark of global capitalist regimes. Manufacturing and assembly jobs have historically been conducted in poor countries benefiting multinational Western corporations without requiring the large-scale migration of labor to the West. Workers without immigration or mobility rights have supported industrial development in the West for over a century. However, rarely in the past have these workers been in voice-to-voice conversation with their faraway customers, and rarely has part of the product being exchanged been a responsive, caring, connected self itself. I argue that two sets of processes structure these new global service workers' jobs. First, a set of relations through which they are distanced from the West and seen as physically remote speakers of a strange version of English who pose a danger to Western economic and national sovereignty. Second, workers are "just like" their customers in the West with the familiarity and ability to connect with clients that are necessary for successful customer service. In reconciling these two processes, workers enter into a complex interplay of colonial histories, class relations, and national interests, which are embedded within their authenticity work. This is the work of being oneself and simultaneously like someone faraway imagines one should be. Becoming a phone clone involves emulating, through voice, an ideal transnational call center worker who is both close to and distant from customers in the West.

This terrain of sameness and difference is exemplified in the June 2006 cover image of *Time* magazine that featured India's predominance in transnational customer service work.[6] The representative of "India Inc.," as the story is titled, is a light-skinned Indian woman, dressed in traditional clothing and wearing ornamental wedding jewelry under her headset. The woman is attractive, and looks straight into readers' eyes. Her confident demeanor defies the image of the passive Oriental other and signifies the new India to which the article refers. At the same time, she is dressed in traditional Indian clothing, complete with the highly eroticized nose ring. She signifies a worker who embraces Western development but does not forget her place in the social hierarchy.[7] This image captures an ideal that Indians employed as transnational service workers emulate. Just like the woman depicted in *Time,* they are strange, yet somewhat familiar to those in the West whom they serve.

In fact, Indian workers are not uniformly fair skinned, and they do not dress in Indian outfits to go to work. Indeed, they are encouraged to dress in Western clothing and be deferential and subservient rather than assertive as depicted in the *Time* image. The image, however, captures the West's ambivalence toward the non-West, which can be traced back to early colonial expansion. Anshuman Prasad and Pushkala Prasad point to the ways in which the non-West is simultaneously weak and threatening to the West. They note that "while colonialism was spurred by the moral imperative to 'improve' the non-West in the West's own image, paradoxically colonialism also evinced an intense desire to preserve the 'authenticity' of the non-West."[8]

The term *authenticity* has historically been associated with culture or art, although I argue that it provides useful insight into transnational service work. On one level, authenticity refers to something that is real and original rather than an imitation, such as a piece of art certified to be produced by an artist. At the same time, authenticity can be used to refer to an accurate representation or copy.[9] For example, the Wilma Cafe in Toronto is marketed as providing "authentic Moroccan cuisine," which is food that is like that found in another faraway place. Significantly, as Theo Van Leeuwen summarizes, "something is authentic because it is declared authentic by an authority."[10] In this sense, the study of authenticity is a study of legitimacy because it both confers value onto that which is deemed authentic and legitimates the position of those who have the right to do the deeming. This is not to suggest that the hierarchy between the authenticated and the authenticator is fixed or clearly visible. Rather, authenticity is continually being constructed and contested. In a fascinating account of Western travelers engaged in eating unfamiliar foods, Jennie Germann Molz provides an example of the negotiated nature of authenticity. In describing their experiences of eating foods such as fried bugs and naming these culinary adventures as "dangerously strange," travelers reify "their own White, Western culture as the norm against which other cultures are defined as exotic and strange."[11] Authenticity, in this sense, serves to establish hierarchies and police boundaries. Transnational service workers negotiate these boundaries and hierarchies through their authenticity work, which involves enacting originality in terms of difference while at the same time reproducing sameness by being an accurate representation.

These ideas on authenticity provide a rich terrain on which to examine the experiences of transnational service workers. Their work is a site where hierarchies are established and boundaries are policed through notions of authenticity. Thus far, much of the discussion of authenticity in relation to customer service work has focused on the rather simplistic notion of being "true to self." Management gurus B. Joseph Pine and James Gilmore, for example, write about the need for organizations to provide customers with an "authentic experience" in the context of the experience economy. They identify "the management of the customer perception of authenticity" as the "new business imperative."[12] This new business imperative requires the provision of service that does not come across as scripted, fake, and insincere. By being themselves, workers can convince customers that they know and care about their real needs. However, when service providers and customers occupy different spatial, cultural, historical, and material landscapes, workers are not asked to be themselves but rather to emulate an ideal as imagined by their employers and customers.

In highlighting workers' efforts to become authentic clones simultaneously enacting sameness and difference, I do not wish to suggest that their work involves merging their "real Indian" selves with a predefined Western "other." Indeed, workers do not, by and large, see their adoption of Western accents and cultures as a loss of Indian identity. Rather, they note that Western customers and clients demand that they sound a particular way, so interactions are "culturally seamless."[13] Accordingly, I explore the experiences of customer service agents in the context of multiple and continual *constructions* of distinctions between India and the West that are made by customers, workers, managers, trainers, policy makers, and the press. Part of the work of being a transnational customer service agent is making sense of, participating in, and negotiating these constructions on a daily basis.

The Distant Server

Capital expansion involves not only the use of existing labor pools but also the creation of workers with defined characteristics and outlooks. Carol Upadhya notes that "the deployment or creation of cultural identities in the service of capital is a dialectic process in which pre-existing cultural communities, gendered identities or racially marked groups are transformed into labor forces that perform particular roles in the production process, which in turn mark these social identities with the stamp of capital."[14] This book explores the ways in which the work experiences and identities of customer service agents in India are shaped by and in turn shape the interactions between Indian workers and Western customers over the phone. The identities of customer service workers in India are continually being formed and reformed through their experiences of their jobs. Their encounters with Western clients serve as sites where ongoing processes of connection and differentiation between India and the West are enacted. Sara Ahmed argues that "through strange encounters, the figure of the 'stranger' is produced, not as that which we fail to recognize, but as that which we have already recognized as 'a stranger.'" Encounters do not simply occur in the present—rather, "each encounter reopens past encounters."[15] It is in the context of India's colonial past that Indians are seen not only as strangers but also as deeply threatening to the sanctity of

Western jobs. Through their daily encounters with Westerners over the phone, Indians are placed outside the dominant nation, often through violent and racist expressions of exclusion on the part of customers. They are called "thieves" for taking jobs away from the West, evoking discourses of stranger danger while simultaneously facilitating the work of Western nation-building.[16]

The construction of Indians as distant occurs therefore, not accidently, in conjunction with the strong public backlash against outsourcing. During the early phases of the large-scale outsourcing of customer service work in the early 2000s, organizations aggressively trained workers to mask their physical location in India. Workers started their shifts by familiarizing themselves with news, traffic, and weather information in their make-believe homes and were also asked to use these to deceive customers about their true location in India. Since around 2005, however, these attempts have been replaced by the open acknowledgment that customer service work is done by Indians who are faraway—distant not only in terms of their physical location but also permanently different in their ways of communicating. This difference assures the security of Western sovereignty since these deficiencies severely curtail excessive capital or labor flight out of the West. In this sense, difference is simultaneously a "site of subject formation" and a social relation, where interactions are determined by histories and practices that "produce the conditions for the construction of group identities."[17] Through their telephone encounters with clients in the West, Indian customer service agents emerge as a distinct group of Indians—highly educated, entrepreneurial, and trainable while at the same time subservient, awkward, and deficient.

The Economy of Familiarity

The social relations of difference are experienced, for customer service workers, in the context of a seemingly contradictory economy of familiarity. Workers' jobs are essentially to serve, which involves the deeply familial work of caring and empathy. Work processes, training, and routines within customer service work are justified in terms of the need for customers to experience workers as familiar. During telephonic encounters, Western customers should feel that their needs have been recognized, they have been cared for, and they can trust the stranger on the phone with confidential information. The success of the Indian call center industry depends fundamentally on Western customers seeing Indian workers as people who are close—close enough to help manage their credit card expenses, understand the best insurance plan in the context of their lives, fix their computers, and identify the most suitable telephone plan for their lifestyles. Customer service agents' work of becoming familiar with their customers involves living on Western time, embracing Western cultures, engaging in accent training to be understood, and practicing to remove the language deficiency, which is termed as their mother tongue influence (MTI). As A. Aneesh has summarized, for Indian customer service workers, "cultural simulation—is the very basis of authentic performance" since call center workers are supposed to sound like their customers in order to make them feel comfortable.[18]

These practices suggest that there remains a fundamental difference between commodities that are material products and voice-to-voice or face-to-face services. Marxist analysis on the fetishism of commodities shows how the labor that goes into the production of goods is mystified so that goods are seen as independent of the labor through which they are produced. In voice-to-voice service work, the product is exchanged via an encounter between two materially situated, socially located individuals—and workers' labor is part of the commodity being exchanged. Desirable workers are not only the cheapest and most productive, as in subcontracted manufacturing or assembly jobs, but also those who are familiar to Western customers. Elaborate recruitment procedures, detailed monitoring processes, and the spatial organization of workspaces serve to produce Indian customer service agents as Western clones—people who talk, think, and act in ways that are familiar to those in the West.

Such cultural cloning involves the reproduction of sameness and facilitates the entrenchment of normative social hierarchies.[19] The stated need for workers to be as much like their customers as possible is used to justify immense organizational control over all spheres of workers' lives. Companies determine the activities their employees should engage in during their leisure time, the ways in which they should speak, the names they should be known by, and the nature of their personal beliefs. Philomena Essed and David Goldberg note that "cultural cloning is predicated on the taken-for-granted desirability of certain types, the often unconscious tendency to comply with normative standards, the easiness with the familiar and the subsequent rejection of those who are perceived as deviant."[20] Through grueling recruitment rounds and training sessions, deviant or inappropriate workers—those who cannot be made identifiable, knowable, and familiar to Westerners—are weeded out. Others are trained to speak in a "neutral" accent. Yet, they are never seen to be "real" speakers of English and this logic of deficiency structures their language training. By virtue of their ethnicity as well as the corrupting influence of local languages, all Indians are deemed to require remedial training to be understood by Westerners.

Providing service requires workers to become both familiar and deferential at all costs, including in the face of overt racism. Customer service is seen to involve not only being someone with whom the customer can identify but also accepting customer racism as the failure to achieve the required closeness. Workers are trained to respond to racism with empathy and caring rather than anger or detachment. Several assumptions are made through which racism in transnational customer service work is masked—customer service work is seen to require a close connection, which is only possible if workers and customers are similar, if workers are cultural clones and therefore easy to identify with. Racism is the effect of workers' failure to become familiar with their customers in the context of the supposedly legitimate national interest of the West to protect jobs and prevent outsourcing.

Authenticity Work

When customer service agents make telephonic contact with Western clients, they immediately begin a process of proclaiming their legitimacy. This effort-filled set of activities, termed *authenticity work,* involves training, learning, and the continual creation of one's identity. Indian customer service agents do authenticity work by simultaneously constructing themselves as foreign workers who do not threaten Western jobs, as legitimate colonial subjects who revere the West, as real Indians who form an offshore model workforce providing the cheap immobile labor needed in the West, as flexible workers who are trainable and global, and as workers who are faraway yet familiar enough to provide good services to their customers.

Based on one hundred interviews with workers at call centers in New Delhi, Bangalore, and Pune, this book explores the authenticity work that forms an integral part of transnational service jobs. Telephone-based customer service centers are part of the ITES (information technology enabled services) industry in India, which is also referred to as the business process outsourcing (BPO) sector. Companies in the ITES/BPO sector include voice-to-voice services as well as back office (email), data entry, and accounting services. Estimates indicate that India holds between 35 percent and 45 percent of the global market in offshore service work. There are currently seven hundred thousand call center workers in India, a sevenfold increase since 2001.[21]

Over the past decade, there has been considerable media coverage on transnational call centers in India. Many reports celebrate the new growth in subcontracting with euphoric enthusiasm and claim, as in an article in the *Statesman,* that it proves that the "Age of India Cometh."[22] Outsourced jobs are said to be fostering a blooming middle class, with benefits trickling down to those who serve the emerging infrastructure and consumer needs. In other reports transnational call center workers are characterized as "cyber-coolies" working in sweatshop conditions.[23] Speaking to workers it becomes clear that these dichotomous perspectives fail to fully capture the experiences of Indian customer service workers.[24] Workers are far from satisfied with and grateful for their so-called comfortable jobs and frequently talk about the stressful and tedious nature of their work. Yet, they do not want the subcontracting trend to end and appreciate their stable incomes and well-organized workspaces. They strive for enriched, interesting work and engage in active processes of decision making in determining how to behave on the telephone, construct themselves, interact with one another, and interpret organizational rules.

Overview of the Book

Two dominant relations structure Indian customer service workers' jobs—(1) the notion that they are fundamentally different from Westerners and (2) the idea that they are their cultural clones and therefore able to establish transnational relationships of familiarity and ease. The chapters in this book highlight the ways in which Indian customer service agents experience these contradictory relations through their training, work processes, and daily interactions with their customers, and the authenticity work which is required as a result. Chapter 1 provides the backdrop for the analysis of workers' experiences and situates the recent growth of India's technology-related service industry within the broader trends of the transnationalization of service work. I argue that the globalization of service work provides unique opportunities to understand the microprocesses of global economic capitalism.[25] In this chapter, I also highlight the methodological approach of studying the global by analyzing the lived experiences of workers. Feminist analysts have focused on the need to move away from grand theories, which characterize globalization as a "meta-myth", a "rape script," or a "narrative of eviction."[26] Instead, we need to focus on the ways in which processes known as global are formed by, and, in turn, form the everyday local lives of individuals. Highlighting the continually contested and heterogeneous nature of global capitalism reveals the microprocesses through which transnational corporate alliances are forged and facilitated. Carla Freeman argues that "not only do global processes enact themselves on local ground but local processes and small scale actors might be seen as *the very fabric of globalization.*"[27] The "fabric" of this book is in-depth interviews with frontline customer service agents in New Delhi, Bangalore, and Pune, conducted between 2002 and 2009. Through these accounts, women and men share their work experiences and describe the ways in which they craft themselves into transnational service workers.

The next segment of the book (Chapters 2 and 3) explores the processes through which Indian customer service agents are constructed as "different" from Westerners. The Indian call center worker is recognized as a "stranger" in the "encounter" between worker and customer; "such encounters allow the stranger to appear, to take form, by recuperating all that is unknowable into a figure that we imagine we might face here, now, in the street."[28] Indian customer service workers are embodied through their voices, and they are known as those who speak a strange and corrupted form of English. Although the availability of a large pool of English-speaking workers is widely cited as one of the main advantages of outsourcing to India, workers are subjected to elaborate training and monitoring processes that are deemed necessary for them to be understood. Becoming a customer service worker involves "sounding right"; this has been termed "aesthetic labor"[29] and is explored in Chapter 2. To understand and be understood by Western customers, workers receive extensive training on "Voice and Accent" and are asked to adjust their pronunciation, grammar, rate of speech, and emphasis. One worker describes the training she received: "What they do is they give you, like, small things like a couple of words, a few words that U.S. people speak in a different way. So instead of we saying 'talking,' they say 't'auking.' So there is a difference. So they kind of teach us these small kind of... they give small tips. This is how you talk. So that the American should understand you."

Aesthetic work occurs in the context of power and hierarchies that are structured not only by organizational processes and individual traits of workers but also by the broader contexts of colonial histories and inequities between nations. In Indian call centers, language serves as a stratification device through which class as well as regional hierarchies between workers are enacted. Even though all Indians are constructed as non-native speakers of English, certain workers (those who are urban, convent-educated, and familiar with Western culture) are deemed to have Mother Tongue Influences (MTIs) that can be "neutralized." These "least different" (or implicitly least deficient) workers are seen to be most appropriate for this industry while the others are unceremoniously shut out.

The universal requirement of voice and accent training serves to entrench the notion that unlike Western customers, Indians are automatically deficient in their use of English. Chapter 3 describes another way in which Indian customer service workers are distanced—in terms of their physical location. Interviews conducted before 2005 reveal that workers were consistently asked to mask their physical location in India. After 2005, however, workers' attempts to hide their locations were largely acknowledged as ineffective, and many agents were asked by their supervisors to openly reveal to their customers that work had been subcontracted to India. Consequently, managing the backlash from customers became part of workers' jobs, and this involves often violent encounters with irate customers who express nationalist protectionism. A trainer recounts Indian agents' dismay at the shift in policy from locational masking to locational transparency because they are now "scared of telling customers they're in India because they think that customers will get wild at them and blast at them." In telephonic encounters, Indians are treated like strangers, outsiders, and thieves.

These "thieves," however, are deemed essential for the success of Western corporations, which have an enormous need for low-cost labor. Business media, trade promotion organizations, and the Indian elite have colluded to construct India as providing the model workforce for IT and ITES outsourcing. In fact, the educational qualifications of Indian customer service workers include bachelor's and master's degrees as well as specialized higher education in engineering or business. Indians may be different from Westerners, but they can be *made* the same through targeted recruitment, careful monitoring, and spatial organization of their work. Chapters 4, 5, and 6 explore strategies through which Indian call center workers are made familiar to their Western customers.

Chapter 4 focuses on the labor processes through which Western work norms are enacted. One woman describes her understanding of the characteristics necessary for success in the call center industry by noting that "you're supposed to be sophisticated, stylish, modern, fashionable, sexy, hot. [You] need to have that talent and skill to impress your trainer, to impress your QC [quality controller], to become at a higher post. Because without doing that you're not going to get anywhere." Becoming this ideal transnational service worker involves a constant process of enacting, revisioning, and resisting distinctions between the West and India, modern and backward, progressive and traditional. This negotiation occurs in the context of three organizational strategies that serve to encourage workers to clone customer accents, attitudes, lifestyles, and outlooks so that they can achieve the connection and closeness required to be successful customer service agents. First, highly competitive recruitment strategies are used to weed out inappropriate workers, and only those who come across as entrepreneurial, trainable, and knowledgeable about Western popular culture are hired. Second, physical workplaces are constructed as Western spaces—which are very different from the local environment. Tall, new, shining, heavily guarded buildings jar against the surrounding crumbling structures and slums. Workers often speak of Indian social spaces as disorderly and unclean in contrast to their highly organized Western workplaces. Third, workers are subjected to monitoring, scripting, and control that are promoted as necessary for them to achieve Western standards of "professionalism." Professionalism involves exacting standards; as one woman reports, "if you don't perform, you're chucked out... it's like that. They follow that six sigma[30] thing very, very strictly. Six sigma is, like, point 999 percentage of error should be there in your quality." Meeting these exacting standards does not, however, mean simply reading accurately from a preset script. One worker highlights the importance placed on the "human touch":

> We have a very stereotype process. We have to follow it. I mean, when you ask me a question, we have a complete website in front of us. And once you ask the question, I have to immediately find the option that your question is related to... [But] I cannot read that out because that is what I have to do. It tells me what I have to do. There are four things I have to do together. I have to listen to you, I have to refer [to the screen], I have to do that thing [what the screen says] and make sure that the dead air between us does not exit ten seconds. I have to keep talking to you. It's a human touch. But during that, if we miss out on anything, then that's a fatal error. And fatal error, straight zero on a call. Now that zero hampers your incentives like anything.

Customer service agents' authenticity work involves providing the "human touch" in the context of a highly structured labor process. Workers also develop creative ways of responding to performance measures by constructing similarity in class terms—they are just like their customers in the West, only much more educated.

Chapter 5 focuses on workers' emotion work of deference and caring, which are central to their jobs.[31] This work involves the enactment of femininity for both male and female employees. Workers serve and care for clients in the West by reproducing hierarchies present in many traditionally feminized service occupations such as nursing and domestic work. Emotion work involves learning to not take the rude behavior of customers personally, maintaining self-worth in the face of abusive customers, and handling rejection. Customer service workers are taught strategies to deal with abusive customers during pre-job and on-the-job training (OJT). Dealing with abuse is recast as a job-related skill, and one customer service worker notes that "communication skill is very important, you know, listening skills is a must. Because if I'm not understanding you, how will I say something to you...you have to react yourself like a very matured person. You cannot sit and cry for each and every thing. If you're abused by a customer, you don't have to sit and cry. You have to react [as] a very understandable person." In line with neoliberal racism,[32] the expression of anger is seen as a customer right while the management of this anger is a worker responsibility. Workers' authenticity work involves understanding, caring for, and connecting with customers who often construct them as thieves and targets of abuse.

A final way in which cultural cloning is facilitated is through time. Chapter 6 focuses on the ways in which workers are required to occupy the same temporal space as their customers. With the time difference of between five and thirteen hours separating Australia, Canada, Britain, or the United States from India, call centers operate primarily during the night. Barbara Adam notes that such an arrangement signifies "colonization with time"[33] where Western clock time is used as the global standard. Indeed, India is promoted as an ideal location for the outsourcing of call center work from the West because the difference in time zones allows companies to provide customer service around the clock. This globalization of clock time makes it seem as though time supersedes localized and embedded material realities. This is far from true for most call center workers, who stress the negative health and social impacts of the schism between their global workplaces and local lives. One call center worker describes her temporal dislocation, saying that during the day, "people are awake, they are mingling...and I am busy sleeping. So I am completely cut out of the world....[At the office] you cannot speak your heart. When you are at home, you have to sleep...So you cannot speak your heart out to them also...sleeping, sleeping, sleeping...You're half-dead." For both women and men, family responsibilities are not assumed to even exist in the context of their night shifts. While their work follows none of the schedules of local industries, schools, and markets, organizational responsibility for households extends only to the transportation of workers between their homes and workplaces. In the meantime, workers manage a host of social and care arrangements to mediate their absences in their local physical settings while dealing with the health implications of waking and sleeping in line with those situated in a distant time zone.

Finally, in the Conclusion, I further develop the notion of authenticity work based on the analysis above, and argue that this important concept provides unique insight into thus far hidden dimensions of the microprocesses of economic globalization. Highlighting this invisible yet crucial work sheds light on the skill and knowledge required of workers in the context of neoliberal economic globalization, as well as on the need for enhanced regulatory protection of worker rights. While customer service work is often designed, presented, and remunerated as repetitive and routinized work, this characterization masks the multitude of multifaceted bridging activities underlying successful customer service in a transnational context. The central aim of this book is to spotlight this authenticity work that, I argue, is the bedrock of the transnational service economy.

1

Transnational Customer Service

A New Touchstone of Globalization

The globalization of customer service work provides a unique opportunity to explore contemporary transnational economic processes. Unlike many other forms of service work where workers and customers interact face-to-face, call center agents are embodied through voice. There are three dynamics that occur in the voice-embodied interactions between Western customers and Indian agents. First, workers enter into a complex set of class politics in relation to their employers, customers, and coworkers. Second, part of their work involves servicing citizenship and negotiating the borders of nations. Third, call center workers engage simultaneously in production and social reproduction through their emotional and aesthetic labor carried through their voices. As a result of the convergence of these dynamics, transnational customer service work serves as a new touchstone of globalization and provides an opportunity to understand contemporary social configurations of race, gender, nationalism, and class.

There has been a dramatic growth in the economic significance of service work globally. The sector has been described as the "great employment sponge"[1] given the sheer number of new service jobs created around the world. As Benjamin Barber summarizes, "services have gone from being the poor cousin of the global economy to being its first citizen."[2] Feminist theorists writing on female-dominated service professions such as teaching, childcare, nursing, and waitressing have historically documented the gendered assumptions implicit in jobs that involve doing things for people as well as the mechanisms through which this work is feminized and often devalued. Many service jobs require the expression of warmth, friendliness, and deference—traits that women are assumed to automatically possess.[3] Women's greater propensity toward servicing is explained in the context of the gendered divisions of household labor and childcare work. Since women have globally and historically been linked with mothering and the domestic sphere, they are assumed to be well practiced in the skills necessary to perform work requiring care and warmth. Gendered assumptions about women's natural ability to be service workers are often based on highly static stereotypes of the differences between women and men that fail to account for the complex ways in which masculinities and femininities are enacted in peoples' daily lives. Yet, it remains an undisputable demographic fact that many service professions continue to be female-dominated. Feminist work that attempts to unpack the links between stratification, femininity, and service work dates back to the 1980s.[4] As Winifred Poster and George Wilson reflect, however, "although many important studies have explored the implications of race, class, and gender of this labor within the Global North, the transnational implications are yet to be detailed in a comprehensive way."[5] This book is part of the growing body of scholarship aimed at addressing this gap.

The large-scale transnational offshoring of service work is a relatively recent phenomenon.[6] Much more prevalent historically has been the movement of service workers with the temporary or permanent migration of domestic workers and health care workers from labor-rich countries to the West. While pockets of service work, such as medical transcription and some software programming, were offshored in the 1970s, it was not until the significant advancement of telecommunication technologies and computer systems in the 1990s that a much larger-scale emergence of the transnational service sector was possible. India, in particular, has experienced a phenomenal growth of the transnational call center sector since the early 1990s. Eighty percent of Fortune 500 companies now outsource some work to India. The growth trajectory of the call center industry in India has been

A Technology Park. Photograph taken by Kiran Mirchandani, 2006

nothing less than spectacular.[7] This dramatic growth has altered the physical and social landscape of many Indian cities. Self-contained technology parks housing tall, gleaming buildings with perfectly manicured lawns have sprouted in all major Indian cities and many smaller urban centers.

What explains the dramatic supersonic growth of this sector in India since the early 2000s? Arjun Appadurai argues that histories create geographies rather than the reverse.[8] Several histories provide elements of the "map" that explains the emergence of this particular sector at this particular moment in India. These histories include the establishment of schooling infrastructure during colonial rule, state economic and immigration policies, and capital investments in the West aimed at cultivating opportunities for lower labor costs.

Mapping the Boom in India's Call Center Industry

India's competitive advantage in global services outsourcing is frequently said to lie in its large, English-speaking workforce. The creation of this indigenous English-schooled population began over four hundred years ago with the emergence of missionary schools and the subsequent colonial policy of the establishment of English-medium schools. Rather than simply teaching language, these schools taught students about the world from colonizers' perspectives. Convent schools served to create the indigenous elite, who would occupy lower-level roles in the colonial administration.[9] The legacy of stratified education continues to dominate the contemporary Indian schooling landscape, with sharp distinctions between the economic outcomes of students from English-medium convent schools, and government-run regional language schools. Colonial legacies, therefore, significantly structure transnational service work given the connection required between worker and customer in the context of the voice-embodied nature of this work. Indeed, as Rosemary Batt and her colleagues have observed, the spread of services is "based on historic linguistic and post-colonial ties: between France and French post-colonial countries such as Morocco and Tunisia; Spain and Latin America; the United Kingdom and Ireland, India and South Africa; and the US and Ireland, India, Canada and the Philippines."[10]

In India, although the English-speaking workforce has been in place for centuries, it is only since the early 1990s that it has been conceived of as a tradable commodity. State policy, both within India and in the West, played a key role in the current manifestation of the transnational customer service industry. Since 1991 the Indian government has pursued an aggressive set of neoliberal reforms aimed at encouraging foreign investment.[11] The information technology and information technology enabled services (IT/ITES) sector has been a key element of state strategy. The state-allied organization the National Association of Software and Services Companies (NASSCOM) was established in 1988 with the specific mandate to promote trade in software and services. The government of India markets the industry through the slogan "Serviced from India," and it continues to provide considerable tax benefits and regulatory flexibility to promote the industry.[12] The Indian state has not only withdrawn from taxing the IT/ITES industry but, more significantly, also from regulating it. There are few enacted and enforced protections in place for workers who individually "bear the brunt" of the sudden cancellation of contracts or closure of firms.[13]

Trade liberalizing policies in the 1990s, often pursued as modernization strategies, were accompanied by a seemingly contradictory emergence of Hindu fundamentalism in the political landscape of India. With the growing influence of the West that accompanied the influx of foreign capital, the rise of the Hindu-oriented Bharatya Janata Party provided a forum for the interplay between Westernization and Indian nationalism. In this context, as Sareeta Amrute argues, "Hinduism became both the vehicle to 'protect' India and one to help Indians solidify through both practices and ideologies equating Hinduism with particular sets of skills—their place in the multinational world of (IT) labor."[14] These skills include the ability to elevate paid work to an expression of one's spiritual service to family and nation. State liberalization policy, in this sense, has facilitated a series of iterative negotiations through which new connections among foreign capital, colonial histories, religious traditions, and local labor have been brokered.

Skill-oriented immigration policies in the West also played a key role in this current rapid expansion of the IT/ITES sector in India. Western companies began outsourcing processes to lower-cost destinations within the United States in the 1960s and 1970s. At the same time, some companies set up offshore branches in response to deregulation and competition to take advantage of labor cost arbitrage.[15] Decades of skill-based immigration policies have led to a well-established Indian diaspora in the West. Highly skilled Indian immigrants began to rise to key positions within Western companies in the United States. These "strategic agents"[16] were well placed to establish software, customer service, and back-office outfits in India. In addition, the growth of offshoring is related to the immigration backlash in the West. The migration of work rather than people facilitates a truce between the needs of the state and the needs of capital in the West. While immigration requires the provision of settlement services and the potential expansion of citizenship, transnational outsourcing allows the state to import the work without the body.[17]

The transnationalization of customer service work was facilitated by the particular structure of this industry that was driven largely by the need for cost rationalization in the West. In the United States, for example, the provision of customer service has shifted from a face-to-face to an on-the-phone mode of delivery. In this shift, the requirement of efficiency often contradicts the need for customer orientation.[18] Efficiencies achieved through automation, standardization, and work speed-up collide with customer expectations of timely, personalized, and accessible service. There is therefore considerable disillusionment with telephone-based service provision, with accompanying measures such as the establishment of "do not call" registries. This, exacerbated by processes such as long waiting times for customers, creates the precondition for hostile customer interactions. In this context, emotion work such as the management of customer anger is often a key element of all call center work.[19] Manifestations of customer anger are affected, however, by the geographical location of workers and customers, the history of these geographies, the nature of the service being provided, and the organizational processes structuring worker-customer interactions.

Labor costs in the West have been reduced not only through the introduction of rationalized telephone-based customer service delivery but also through the organizational strategy of subcontracting. Subcontracting was established over the past half century as an effective method to minimize labor costs. In the 1960s, large U.S. companies began to move their back-office processes from their headquarters in major urban centers to smaller Midwestern towns where labor was abundant and unionization rates were low. The proliferation of reengineering in the 1990s facilitated the standardization of processes that made the movement of work even easier. This was accompanied by technologies such as the automatic call distribution system through which calls could be seamlessly transported across geographical sites. In fact, U.S. companies experimented with setting up operations in India as early as the 1960s, far before the current mass migration of IT/ITES work.[20]

In the 1990s, with the impending doom of the Y2K bug, the IT industry in India flourished, and dozens of large local Indian companies were well-established to receive outsourcing contracts from the West. The software slowdown in the West in the early 2000s occurred in the context of the already established outsourcing of a wider range of activities, broadly termed business process outsourcing (BPO). Recessionary pressures in the West in fact bolstered the industry, and by 2002, annual growth of the sector in India was 70 percent.[21] Much before this expansion, the Indian state played a key role in fostering outsourcing through both economic policy and the liberalization of its telecom policy. Rather than universalizing telephone access, this measure allowed foreign companies to build infrastructure in India explicitly for the purposes of transnational businesses.[22] As a result there are vast discrepancies between the gleaming buildings within which transnational call centers are housed and their surrounding spaces.

Uneven Development. Photograph taken by Kiran Mirchandani, 2008

The Indian government traditionally provided tax advantages to software and technology-based companies. Paul Davies argues that the construction of an affiliation between IT work (which includes programming), and BPO (which includes any work involving even peripheral use of a computer) was a stroke of marketing genius: "IT services exported from India were in a zero tax regime. Potentially BPO offshore would be treated as just another Indian industry and would have to pay tax. It was therefore far less attractive.... The answer lay at hand. It was a four-letter acronym, ITES. This handy little collection of tax-avoiding capital letters actually stands for IT-enabled services."[23] Tax benefits therefore have allowed companies to set up call centers in India at considerably lower costs. With the significant cost advantages, firms not offshoring their customer service work are seen to hold a place of considerable disadvantage vis-à-vis their competitors who have. A study by a large consulting company characterizes outsourcing as an inevitable necessity in the contemporary economic environment, noting that "for every $1 that is offshored the company gains 58 cents in net cost reduction even as they gain a better (or identical) level of service. In other words, companies that have so far failed to shift operations to India—whether it is software development, IT systems integration, customer support, back office work, or personnel management—will be at a large and growing competitive disadvantage."[24] The production of this sense of the inevitability of outsourcing to India is an orchestrated social accomplishment, involving agents enacting histories, policies, and economies. Indeed, as the chapters to follow attest, transnational call centers are sites of colonial domination, patriarchal reification, identity construction, worker resistance, management control, and racist expression—occurring simultaneously—through overt work processes and normative subtexts in place. In these sites, workers negotiate these relations in their daily lives and perform invisible yet vital authenticity work in order to hold the tension between diverse and divergent forces. The unique position of transnational customer service workers, which makes them an emerging touchstone of globalization, rests in their location on the multiple borders of class, nation, and production.

Working Borders

Class Borders

Call center workers straddle the class borders of professional and routinized work. They are neither traditional blue-collar workers, even though they work in highly repetitive and controlled jobs, nor are they white-collar workers engaged in creative knowledge production.[25] Yet, in the Indian context, call center workers are part of the elite transnational technology-related sector and are closely associated with the emergence of the new middle class.[26] Customer service agents therefore occupy shifting and often ambiguous class borders. Their work is constructed as "professional" and yet work processes involved are highly routinized. In addition, the work requires servitude and deference, and allows for little worker discretion. Like their managers they connect directly with customers abroad and are intimately connected to the global economy. Yet they earn considerably less than business owners and managers and share job features that are typical of lower-level jobs.[27] Workers are not only producers but also occupy an important social position as India's new consumers. As Leela Fernandes argues, India's new middle class is epitomized in those involved in IT/ITES jobs in terms of both their access to wealth and the lifestyle of consumption. The growth of call centers in India has increased the disposable income of middle-class youth who are simultaneously the producers as well as an important force behind the proliferation of consumerism.[28]

Class borders are also transnationally crossed in daily worker-customer encounters. Unlike in the West where many call centers often offer poorly paid, part-time, or temporary precarious jobs, Indian workers have salaries that are higher than those offered in local industries. They have full-time jobs and benefits such as transport or health services. While customer service work involves deference and servitude on the part of the customer service agent, class hierarchies between workers and customers are far from static. Indian call center workers highlight their higher educational qualifications and class positions vis-à-vis their Western customers, not all of whom are as highly educated.

In these ways, careful attention to the experiences of customer service workers sheds light on the lived and experiential nature of class relations. Class is a social relation rather than one's place in a predetermined structure of hierarchies. As Diane Reay explains, "what it means to be middle or working class, black or white, female or male shifts and changes, not only from one historical era to another, but for individuals over time as they negotiate the social world."[29] Class negotiation is a central and continuous part of customer service work.

Citizenship Borders

A. Aneesh characterizes transnational service work as "virtual migration" with a very different relationship to the nation compared to more conventional forms of labor migration. He notes that under the system of virtual migration, "labor bypasses the state borders while the immigrants' body stays within national temporal spaces."[30] Workers therefore migrate and remain simultaneously and, in this, perform border work in relation both to the nation to which they migrate and the nation within which they stay. Part of this border work is individually pursued, such as efforts to maintain self-esteem in the face of customer racism through expressions of nationalism, but a large part of border work is also seen as a job requirement. Workers are required to adopt a Western accent, use an alias, and become familiar with Western popular culture. This organizationally mandated "national identity management"[31] occurs in the context of colonialism and racism.[32]

Transnational corporations have historically always depended on racialized "othering" to lower wages in order to justify protectionism. There are numerous examples of the links between globalization and racialization, such as assumptions made by employers that Chinese workers are satisfied with the low wages they receive because they would otherwise be getting less, or that labor in the West must be protected from large labor pools interested in performing their jobs without making any claims for quality of work.[33] The transnationalization of services provides the opportunity for continuity in these forms of racialization and opens up new avenues for its reinforcement and resistance. It allows for anonymous customer expressions of nationalism and racism within the context of structural economic inequities between employers, customers, and workers. These structural inequities, however, are enacted, interpreted, and resisted as a part of workers' jobs.

A key part of the work of servicing national borders for workers involves representing India to the world in a way that protects and enhances offshoring. This representation evokes a rhetoric of traitors and ambassadors, which is sprinkled through training programs, media reports, and workplace discourses. On one hand, state branding practices have to be enacted over the phone by workers who are seen as the frontline ambassadors of Brand India. On the other hand, attempts to raise issues about exploitation are seen as undermining the economic prosperity of the nation. For example, Pramod Bhasin, the CEO of an outsourcing provider, is quoted as responding to reports of poor working conditions by saying, "[T]he world is praising the Indian IT Industry... But we are bent on killing the golden goose."[34] The "we" are not all Indian workers, but rather just the traitors among "us."

Production Borders

Indian call center workers continually straddle the borders between production and social reproduction. Kathi Weeks summarizes this duality in service work: "processes of production today increasingly integrate the labors of the hand, brain, and heart as more jobs require workers to use their knowledge, affects, capacities for cooperation and communicative skills to create not only material but increasingly immaterial products."[35] These connections between production and reproduction fundamentally structure transnational service workers' daily lives. Workers' attitudes and personalities are part of the service that they provide, and workers are required to reproduce themselves in particular ways.[36] As Reena Patel observes, "unlike silicon chip production in Taiwan, maquiladoras in Mexico, or McDonald's in France, transnational customer service employment represents a shift from exporting the *production* of material goods or culture to a full scale *reproduction* of identity and culture. In contrast to McDonald's selling french fries in Paris, but not requiring an American accent from its French employees, call center operations are based on the availability of workers trained to embody an American identity and cultural cues."[37]

As part of their jobs, workers perform a host of emotional labor for which they draw on their socialization, perspectives, and experience. Feminist scholars have long highlighted the embodied nature of service work; however, much of the analysis of emotional labor is based on the body, while customer service agents interact with their voices rather than their bodies. Workers' bodies are carried through their voices, and, in this context, workers are trained to speak and sound in particular ways to their customers.

Call center work also depends on a complex infrastructure through which workers' family and home responsibilities can be met. This is particularly significant because call center workers in India perform part or all of their jobs during the nighttime. Employees depend on parents and in-laws as well as on domestic help for childcare and housework.[38] The normalization of night work and the lack of state and organizational responsibility for workers' temporal dislocation have resulted in a gendered incorporation of low-paid service workers who provide the invisible support for the industry. Saskia Sassen observes, "professional households need to function like clockwork...[T]hese households should be reconceptualized as part of [the infrastructure of global cities] and the low-wage domestics as strategic infrastructure maintenance workers."[39]

Their location within the multiple borders of class, nationalism, and production makes call center workers an important group to study. Much can be learned about the workings of globalization from workers' reflections on their social and economic contexts. Transnational customer service work provides a fascinating site for analysis insofar as it brings to the fore class relations, national hierarchies, and work norms, all of which are experienced, created, reconciled, and reformed repeatedly through daily voice encounters between workers and customers. In addition, a unique feature of service work is the direct contact between worker and customer which transforms the traditional dyadic worker-management relationship into a three-way connection between management, workers, and customers.[40] Because of the synchronous nature of customer service work, the nature of the "product" being bought and sold depends not just on the service provider but also on the recipient. Service work can never be fully automated because it involves a collaborative interaction between worker and customer.[41] Given that a large proportion of customer service work now occurs remotely, call centers are an important site to understand dynamics that underlie many forms of service work.[42] As Margaret Abraham summarizes, the call center industry "epitomizes some of the key contemporary issues concerning the shifting of work, labor relations, economic development, and regulation."[43]

Meeting Workers

A multiyear interpretive study is necessarily a journey in methodological discovery. Rather than a preplanned agenda, data collection for this book was driven by issues requiring further exploration at each stage. In five separate trips between 2002 and 2009, one hundred interviews were conducted in New Delhi, Bangalore, and Pune.[44] The central criterion that framed the data collection was that frontline workers' experiences—anonymously shared—would form the bedrock of the study. During the first two trips, call center workers were contacted through local networks of friends and colleagues. Out of the fifty-eight interviews conducted in Delhi and Bangalore in 2002 and 2004, nine were with workers who had advanced to team leader or trainer positions, and five were with managers. Although these interviews with managers, team leaders, and trainers provided interesting information about work processes and industry structure, they seemed to regurgitate much of what was published in marketing and promotional materials produced by companies and in circulation in the business media. The remaining forty-four interviews with frontline customer service agents who spent their work days answering calls were much more informative.

After the call center industry in large Indian urban IT forerunners such as Delhi and Bangalore was well-established, companies began to set up centers in smaller Indian cities where they could access more workers. As a smaller city, Pune provided a fascinating example of this trend in light of its history as India's education center. Since around 2005, Pune has experienced significant growth in the call center sector.[45] City officials promote Pune as a "global city" with technical educational institutions and corporate group head offices. For this book, thirty-six interviews were conducted in Pune in 2006, 2007, and 2009—except for two (one manager and one quality analyst, both had started as customer service representatives), all these interviews were with frontline call center workers. Overall, interviews in Pune raised fascinating issues related to training, regional accents, and the effects of the industry on local development. To further understand the ways in which the "right" workers for call center work were being selected, six additional interviews were conducted with workers who had been shortlisted numerous times for call center jobs but had been repeatedly unsuccessful in getting jobs in the industry. Some of these workers were working in back-office jobs.

The analysis in this book draws primarily on the seventy-eight interviews with frontline call center workers, although the remaining interviews are referred to where appropriate. All respondents work with organizations serving U.S. and U.K. clients, with a handful in Australian or Canadian processes. These regions where the clients were located are broadly referred to as the "West" in this book. This term is used in conjunction with the historical theorizing in postcolonial scholarship on the ideological hierarchies between the "West" and the "rest"; rather than separate geographical entities, these terms represent concepts that are continually being defined in relation to one another.[46] As explored in following chapters, workers in India continually experience and define the "West" through their interactions with customers on the phone.

During the first couple of years of data collection, call center workers were contacted via friends and colleagues in India. Finding people who knew someone who worked in a call center was not difficult. I noticed that workers, however, were interested and conscious of the perspectives of the person through whom they had come to be involved. For example, some workers had been told about the project by colleagues in their organizations or by their relatives. For others, parents or roommates were within earshot during interviews. I realized that despite confidentiality and anonymity protocols in place, snowballing techniques and home-based interviews did not allow workers to remain fully anonymous. From 2006 on, therefore, I abandoned snowball recruitment and instead relied on newspaper advertisements. Through classifieds, I invited workers to share their experiences in confidential and anonymous interviews. For this purpose, I set up an office that was centrally located but not too close to any call center. All respondents in this study received a small honorarium that was primarily to cover their transportation costs.

Had I been less committed to providing a safe and anonymous forum for respondents to share their views, data collection could have proceeded in many other ways that may have also generated useful knowledge. I often resisted the impulse to interview managers or request entry into organizations where I could conduct participant observations. It may have been useful to witness training programs or recruitment sessions. However, all these approaches require organizational sanction, which I believed would undermine respondents' perception of the autonomy of this project.

I started interviews by informing workers that I was not in contact with management officials at any company, and I followed through on this commitment. Beyond the few interviews in initial years with managers, managerial viewpoints were drawn primarily from sources in the public domain. The focus of the project thus remained not on the work structures, processes, and norms in place but rather on workers' *lived experiences* of these. Indeed, with a clear sense of the worker-focused nature of this study, respondents were extremely forthcoming. Although not formally solicited, confidential materials such as company correspondence, training manuals, notes on work processes, performance appraisals, and recruitment letters were shared by many respondents. In one case, I had the opportunity to interview the same person twice (two years apart), but all the other respondents were interviewed only once.

Interviews were in-depth, qualitative conversations, and respondents were encouraged to describe their backgrounds, career orientations, work habits and interests, employment conditions, training experiences, feelings toward their jobs, family lives, and career aspirations. Workers were asked to tell stories about their past, to recount instances which had a significant impact on their work lives, and to explain their actions and feelings. The purpose of the interviews was to understand how workers made sense of their working lives and the social and organizational structures within which they were embedded. Workers were also encouraged to reflect historically on how they came to be working where they now were.[47] Rather than an interest in the generalizability of results, the aim of the study was to gain understandings of how people understood and experienced their work processes. During these interactions, workers were not "at work," and this is clearly reflected in the often casual language of the interviews, which are sprinkled with Hinglish[48] and colloquialisms used in casual conversations—these language peculiarities are reproduced and should not be considered grammatical errors in the quotes presented throughout this book. Indeed, the extensive use of quotes serves to give voice to workers' off-the-phone selves.

Almost all the seventy-eight frontline call center workers interviewed were single and in their twenties. Three workers were over thirty, and nine were married or engaged. In addition, most respondents had bachelor's degrees and several had master's degrees or additional diplomas. Interestingly, however, this tendency toward higher education was much lower in interviews conducted after 2006 when many workers reported that they started their jobs after completing high school. In terms of their compensation, workers earned between INR 5,500 and INR 30,000 per month (US$120–US$650). Entry-level workers in international call centers earn three times the monthly Indian per capita wage. They earn twice as much as high school teachers, accountants, or marketing professionals with a graduate degree.[49] Workers earn a fraction of the earnings of their counterparts doing similar work in the West, although wage differentials between Western and Indian call center workers are reported to be diminishing with the increasing prominence of immigrant workers in low-wage call center jobs in the West.[50] Of the seventy-eight frontline call center workers interviewed for this project, forty-three were men and thirty-five were women.

Nature of Jobs

There was remarkable breadth in the nature of workers' jobs in terms of the processes in which they worked. Many jobs were related to providing customer service in the IT and banking sectors. This included dealing with customers who called toll-free numbers with hardware or software computer-related problems or difficulties with their Internet connections and phones. A few jobs required workers to make calls in order to sell cellular telephone plans. In banking, jobs involved dealing with credit cards or loans, and workers addressed inquiries, payments, and collections. Several jobs were related to selling or servicing life or vehicle insurance, making airline reservations or dealing with lost baggage, and providing support for catalogue sales. Despite the diversity of job titles (such as customer care executive, technical support specialist, collections agent, process associate, customer advisor, subject matter expert), all respondents had jobs that involved providing service to customers. Many were involved in "repair work," defined as "fixing things that have gone wrong between organizations and their publics."[51]

Researchers have noted that organizations often outsource their least complex service requirements based on the assumption that simple transactional work requires minimal contextual knowledge.[52] On one level, this rang true in workers' characterization of their processes as providing technical support, addressing billing inquiries, providing loan information, or taking orders. At the same time, as workers discussed the actual tasks they completed, it became clear that the distinction between complex and routine tasks may accurately explain factory work but translates poorly to customer service jobs. Workers reported that there were an infinite number of issues that could come up around a seemingly simple request. For example, those in charge of collections received detailed customer histories that they were then required to translate into an appropriate collection strategy based on their understanding of organizational rules, customer resources, and established timelines. Workers whose jobs were classified as "technical support" reported that this involved assessing customers' technological skills before a solution could be proposed, managing customer anxiety if they were not familiar with their machines, and judging which troubleshooting steps may generate feelings of incompetence and anger. Also under the rubric of technical support, some workers dealt with customers who had called to cancel their service—these processes were termed "saves" and involved providing technical resolutions, explanations for why prior service had been poor, and special offers that would induce customers to stay with the company. Many jobs involved both sales and service. For example, workers who took catalogue sales orders also listened to customers' needs to assess whether other products would be more appropriate. Workers receiving calls from customers whose Internet service was not working were asked to end calls by making an attempt to ask customers to purchase an enhanced plan. Workers dealing with vehicle loans had to assess the impact of accidents, shifts in ownership, and geographical changes to address balance inquiries. Many workers described their work as requiring "multitasking"—listening to customers, reviewing information, communicating, and recording—all of which need to be done simultaneously, repeatedly, and under significant time pressure.

Demographic Diversities

Tracing the growth of the call center sector in India over the past decade, two consequences of the branding of call center work as highly desirable are discernable. First, such branding, in conjunction with relatively lucrative pay scales, has led to a flight from traditionally middle-class professions in India such as government, law, banking, and sales. Second, opportunities in the sector have led to an incentive for convent-educated, English-speaking youth, particularly those with financial needs, to work in conjunction with, or at times instead of, completing their higher education. These trends have created significant diversity within the call center workforce.

Of the seventy respondents interviewed between 2002 and 2006, all but two had a minimum of bachelor's degrees, and, in many cases, they were also engaged in postgraduate education. Of the thirty individuals interviewed between 2007 and 2009, however, eighteen had completed only high school education before beginning their jobs in call centers. This change suggests a significant impact of the transnationalization of services on the higher education sector in India. Those attempting to complete degrees were doing so by aiming for minimally passing grades without attending classes. For example, one woman explained that she was pursuing a degree in Hindi because "that was the quickest option." She further elaborates on her educational choice: "I'm doing this just to get the certificate and, you know, to make sure that people at least keep their mouth shut and don't give me the excuses."

Several respondents were continuing their education while working, either through correspondence courses or by making special arrangements with instructors to be excused from classes entirely. Workers note that as long as they handed in assignments and passed exams they were able to continue their degrees. Many requested planned leave for a few days prior to exams and covered the entire year's syllabus during their leave, relying on notes from friends. One respondent explains: "We cannot attend the regular classes. Those classes are normally during the daytime. Because they do work and we will be sleeping at that time. We cannot go for the regular colleges." Another describes her routine:

> I am still studying...my classes are in the morning, nine o'clock. So once I come back from job and all, I have my cab at 7:30 a.m., I reach 8:15 a.m. So I have, you know, forty-five minutes to get fresh and all. Then come attend the lectures. [Pause] Hardly, I attend the lectures...hardly matters in a college. You just pay the fine, some take 300, 400, [rupees] and whatever is the fine. You know, the criteria of our college is we just have to submit our practicals [written work] on time. So, we do that. That's it. Everyone at least from my group, we do a job and then we submit our practicals on time.

It is ironic that while Indians are branded by the state as ideal transnational service workers as a result of their high education, they may, in fact, no longer fully fit this profile.[53] This is perhaps not surprising given that workers unanimously note that they are seldom expected to apply the skills or knowledge acquired during their higher education in their jobs. More significantly, many display a profound disengagement from education because of their long hours devoted to work.

The widely promoted stereotype that call center workers are highly educated middle-class youth whose income is spent primarily on luxury consumer goods also masks the economic diversity within the workforce. Several women and men interviewees described significant financial challenges. One woman migrated from Goa to Pune to work in a call center after completing high school because she needed to support her family: "Since my dad was not working. I remember my mom and dad, they were staying [pause]. There was no electricity in the flat. The owner of the flat he would cut electricity...I want to take a house, you know, it's better...My sister is in schooling. She's in 10th standard [grade] now. I want my brother to study. He just did his 11th." A male agent whose father had fallen ill and was unable to work also stopped his education in order to support his parents and sibling: "After 12th, I wanted to continue but couldn't because I had to support my family. So, I was trying both to complete my education as well as to work somewhere. But then, I had to discontinue my education and start working." Workers with significant financial pressures reported feeling that they had few other alternatives to generate a living wage:

> In the year 2004, when my dad got retired, I got graduated.... I was the only earning member in my family. I had to support my family, so I just joined a call center. So, prior to call center, I was working as an office assistant. But the pay was not very good. And in India, the thing is that call centers give the highest pays. Ultimately, the job profile is, like, you have to sit with that headphone and you have to listen to all the yellings and it's very frustrating and psychologically... pressurized. Now I have taken a home loan and... many responsibilities on my shoulders. So, I think that I have to continue with the same job.

The call center sector also accommodates runaway professionals who describe their incomes in other professions as unsustainable given the rising cost of living in India. One worker, for example, practiced law for five years before realizing that his income (INR 5,000 monthly) would never allow him to purchase a home or properly support his family. Another worker with an MBA left a marketing post due to the low pay and constant travel requirements. A homeopathic doctor reported earning only one and a half thousand rupees a month [US$32] after a seven-year doctorate. A vice-principal in a school left his job after seven years to increase his monthly income from INR 7,000 to INR 12,000. These workers' experiences point to the growing group of call center agents who do not fall into the category of youth seeking temporary money-making opportunities for discretionary purchases. These workers are cogently able to identify the simultaneous advantages and drawbacks of call center jobs, and many express a degree of entrapment in the call center work despite descriptions of their proactive strategies to enter the sector.

The conversations with workers reported in this book reflect the complexities of customer service work. Drucilla Barker and Susan Feiner cogently summarize that the usefulness of interpretive approaches lies in the opportunity to highlight "tensions between the material and the representational, between power and knowledge, between the subject as constituted through discourse and the subject as capable of resistance and agency."[54] The phenomenon of the transnationalization of service work provides a touchstone of globalization insofar as it involves a direct and immediate contact between workers and customers occupying different national spaces. The lived experiences of customer service agents in India highlight the ways in which global economic regimes are continually under formation.

2

Language Training

The Making of the Deficient Worker

> I didn't have a neutral accent. I had a mother tongue influence in my accent earlier because we weren't so conscious about our accent and all earlier...[I] never made it a point when I was in school to improve the accent or neutralize it...I didn't know that the accent has to be neutralized. I didn't know that, I thought whatever I'm speaking is correct as far as my grammar is correct. But later on when I moved [to this job], I knew a lot of things that I should have been saying.

In the minute-long conversations that Indian workers have with customers in the West, lifelong identities and century-long histories are evoked. Sara Ahmed observes that identities are constantly constituted and reconstituted in daily meetings with others. In encounters that arise out of colonial histories, as is the case with transnational service work, the connections between those involved in the dialogue is necessarily unequal.[1] The worker quoted above knows himself as deficient in his English language only because he is paid to provide customer service to customers in the West. In this chapter, I explore the extensive language training that prospective customer service agents in India undergo before they are allowed to interact with Western customers. This training is justified in terms of the need for Western clients to understand and be understood by workers. Significantly, however, it also serves to establish a starting point of difference, where all Indians, irrespective of their location, background, or education, are deemed deficient in their use of English. English is claimed as the language of the West. It is in this context that the discourse of "neutrality" and "mother tongue influence" is naturalized.

The identification of those most appropriate for transnational service work involves the enactment of colonial hierarchies shaped by class and regional divisions. This is the search for workers who can do the aesthetic work of looking or sounding right for a particular job. Aesthetic labor represents the "mobilization, development and commodification of embodied 'dispositions' [which]...are to some extent possessed by workers at the point of entry into employment."[2] Through recruitment and training in Indian call centers, ideal workers are identified as those who can be trained to "sound right" to Western customers. There is, however, little clarity on the professional or technical qualifications that workers need to possess to "sound right" in transnational call centers. In fact, there are no universal selection criteria in terms of subjects of study or prior training for call center workers beyond the stipulation that they should possess a university degree or a high school certificate and be proficient in English. Language proficiency, however, is a slippery notion. Although operationalized in training programs as appropriate accent and rate of speech, diction is deemed correct or incorrect in relation to real and imagined encounters between workers and clients. One woman notes:

> The basic idea is that those people should understand you...So this was the main motive behind learning all accent skills...Many a times people are very happy, and those people [say] "how is it possible that staying in India you can speak such good English?"...But at times people are so rude—"Oh, let me talk to someone who can speak English! I just cannot understand you." We get customers like this also. One call, the customer is saying, "Oh, you have fabulous English, you speak so well." And other call you get, "Oh my God! Let me talk to someone who can speak English."

A customer service worker in India is required to be someone who a faraway person in the West can intuitively and automatically understand. Customer comprehension is seen to flow from certain predefined language skills, such as the ability to speak slowly and enunciate in a particular manner. Through the discourse of skill,[3] responsibility for being understood, as well as its failure, is borne largely by the individual worker in India. Workers, however, do not experience such a direct equivalence between speaking in a particular way and customer understanding. As noted by the woman quoted above, Western customers exercise their privilege by naming appropriate and inappropriate English language speakers.[4] Effectively,

Indians know themselves either as deficient in English *because of their location in India* or as proficient in English *despite their location outside the West.*

The link between English and the West is naturalized not only during calls but also through institutionalized language training that workers receive. Training programs serve to bridge the gap between speaking styles in India and the West, but they simultaneously entrench stereotypical differences between Indian and Western speech patterns. Anshuman Prasad and Pushkala Prasad have documented this organizational construction of difference by analyzing training programs in a wide range of global organizations. They observe that training sessions are often "organizational locations for the construction of otherness through the systematic transformation of images about self and the other that markedly echo the legacy of colonialist discourses."[5] Training in Indian call centers, first and foremost, focuses on the universal deficiencies of Indians' use of English. Workers recount:

> The training is basically divided into two parts, one is communication skills training, and the other is process training. Communication skills, basically it means that you have to develop, it is basically getting the American accent, because we, as Indians, we have to have a neutral accent. If somebody has an MTI—Mother Tongue Influence—it is getting out of that to a neutral accent, and then into an American accent. It's basically to get, you know, if you are talking with your customers, the customers should not feel that they are talking to an Indian, that's why we change our names also. We use names like John and Jack.

> For rate of speech, we are given a pamphlet and we are asked to read from the pamphlet. Now within one minute wherever we stop we are given a rating. If it is within 90 to 120 words a minute, it is considered ideal. If it is more then they told me to read more and more things, and they told me to record my voice...I had an [American brand] cell phone, and I used to call their customer service and speak like an American. If they used to understand me then I was very happy. If not, I used to call, think of another problem, and call them again. So that way I used to get practice with that. If they say, "Sorry sir, I cannot understand you, can you please repeat," I used to get a hint that, okay, my rate of speech is high.

Voice exercises such as practicing English during leisure time are a job requirement. Through the discourse of skill, training aims to shift workers from limited to proficient transnational communicators. However, it does so by clearly reinforcing the normative superiority of two kinds of English: the one spoken in the West and the other spoken by the convent-educated, Indian elite. While the stated objective of training programs is to move workers toward an accent identified with the Indian elite (termed a "neutral" accent), the practice of language training often valorizes British or American accents. Claire Cowie's interviews with language trainers in the training industry in India reveal that many of the older trainers who were former English teachers promoted English spoken by convent-educated Indians rather than American accents, whereas younger trainers did the reverse.[6] In either case, deficiency structures the language training of Indian workers because even workers from elite backgrounds are required to undergo substantial periods of language training to ensure

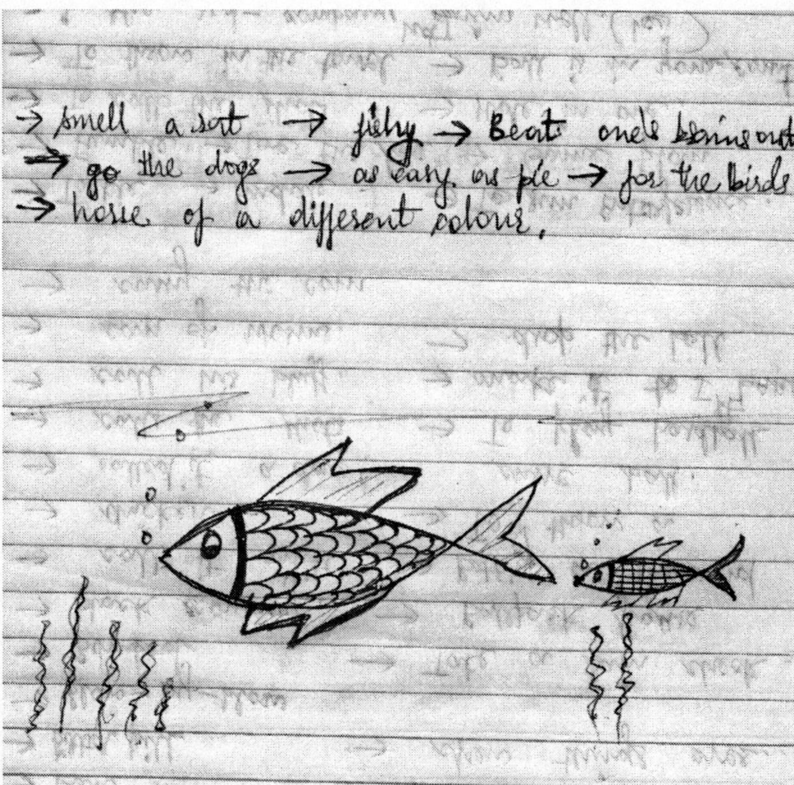

Little Fish Following Big Fish.Drawing provided by respondent.

that they speak in ways familiar to Westerners. While learning to speak in particular ways, workers also need to avoid challenging customers' linguistic superiority. In theory, the stated aim of language training is mutual understanding; however, in practice, Indians are named as needing to engage in learning and training in order to understand and be understood. In this context, training serves to reinforce the differences and reify the hierarchies between workers and customers, Indians and Westerners. During training, one worker who shared her training notes drew an image that cogently captures this subtext. The topic of discussion was idioms such as "fishy." The text accompanying the image has little coherence, suggesting rote note-taking while the image clearly captures the sentiment being conveyed through this requirement to learn phrases assumed to be commonly used by Westerners.

Neutralizing Accent and Correcting Rate of Speech

Anne Witz and her colleagues note that "through the embodied performance of interactive service work, the physical capital of employees is valorized and converted into economic capital by and for organizations."[7] Training programs signify an organizational investment in workers, who are the public face of the organization.[8] Training is also used to eliminate employees unable to achieve the correct embodied performance. The process of being converted into organizational capital, however, is one that is both valorizing and stressful for workers. As one agent notes:

> They are spending too much on training on us. Because they are just flinching you like anything that you are able to communicate with the people who are sitting seven hours apart of you. They are very particular that if you are not able to score that 85+ [performance score], you are kicked out of the company in C-SAT (Customer Satisfaction)... so after the six weeks of training one week, there is one week of transition, that is the customers are calling you and you are sitting live on calls. And you need to clear that as well for a week. If you're through, you're ready to go ahead. If you're not through, you are out of the company.

These images of call center training programs as battlefields where workers are continually being "flinched" reinforce the context of threat under which skill acquisition occurs and the dire consequences of failure.

In the context of training, the process of learning to speak to foreign clients is termed "accent neutralization" and "correcting rate of speech." These goals are significant in the context of the history of the English language in India where English was both the language of the colonizers and intrinsically linked to local, indigenous struggles. Binoo John traces India's long engagement with the English language, which dates back to the arrival of the East India Company in the seventeenth century. Over a century ago, colonialists lamented the corruption of Indian English due to the commonplace practice of language merging in speech and writing. Attempts to correct pronunciation have been part of the age-old civilizing mission, which, much like the training that contemporary transnational customer service workers receive, focused on the correct and incorrect pronunciation of letters.[9]

Although seen in some circles as the language of the British, English usage in India ironically increased dramatically after independence. This significant increase was in part because English figured as a common external language in light of opposition to the government-imposed attempts to universalize the use of Hindi over regional languages. This universalization of the Hindi language was opposed by many Indian states, particularly in the south because Hindi was more prevalent in the north. While English was widely used in commerce, the independent Indian government faced several challenges in attempts to establish English as the universal language of the new nation because of its historical association with the colonizers. As John summarizes, "out of this conflict was born... Indian-English... [which] is well set to rule the country, having defeated the Queen's English in a centuries-long battle."[10] Indian English, or Hinglish, comprises unique word-meanings as well as the comfortable coexistence of words and grammars from various languages in single sentences in both spoken and written language in India.

It is in the context of this merger of English, Hindi, and regional languages that the primary focus of language training for the language neutralization of Indian customer service agents is the removal of "mother tongue influences" and "Indianisms." In the face of this ancient struggle, Shehzad Nadeem quotes a language trainer in Mumbai who notes that customer service agents require extensive training because "schools do not concentrate on phonetics enough and so they pick up sounds from their mother tongue. We teach them to get rid of their mother tongue influence."[11] Indeed, one worker who was unsuccessful in several interviews reflects that he likely had "Hindi fillers" and sought to remove them: "I realized that it was my mistake, the Hindi words, I used to fill up... I decided that I have to conquer all this... I always spoke to my friends in English over the phone. Whenever I used to call them, I used to say. 'You speak in English, I will also speak in English.'" Not all workers are equally convinced of the necessity to correct their ways of speaking. One woman describes the experience of being taught English using preschool pedagogical techniques and curricula, despite the fact that she had completed an undergraduate degree in an English-medium setting:

> For the accent training, we were being taught by cassettes. We had a special trainer—he was singing songs and listening to some conversations. And then we were made to see some movies and stuff. We were actually taught by cassette and we had to repeat all things like they do in nursery standards [schools], repeating the "Aa, Puh, Tuh, Duh" and things like that. It was, you know, a bit funny at that time, we all used to laugh our guts out.[12] What nonsense is this! You know, at times, you feel so frustrated. It's OK, the way we speak is the way we speak. Why do we have to learn such stuff? Then we were told. The basic idea is that those people should understand you.

Language itself is a form of labor in the context of the need to mimic predefined authentic speakers.[13] This labor is facilitated by the now well-established language training industry in India. The labor involved in language learning is vividly displayed in the assessment tools and training materials given to all new recruits. These materials form the basis of "communication skills" courses that typically span from two to six weeks of full-time training. These are supplemented by widely available "self-help" books specifically targeted at call center workers such as *Speak Right for a Call Center Job!, Winning @ Call Center: Confessions of a Calling Agent,* and *Preparing for Call Center Interviews.*[14]

Oddly, the structure of language training for Indian call centers contains many parallels to curricula aimed historically to increase the access of poor and rural Indians to English. One example can be found in the Rapidex English Speaking Course, invented in 1976. This book is estimated to have sold ten million copies to date.[15] The book contains lesson plans through which non–English-speakers can learn English in sixty days. The most recent version comes with an interactive compact disc

(CD). Adopting a highly instrumental approach to language learning, the Rapidex method involves the identification of key phrases that can then be memorized and repeated. While Rapidex was originally targeted toward non–English-speaking and rural populations, this is the same process used to train customer service agents, most of whom have undergone twelve to twenty years of English-medium education. Training books and manuals contain page upon page of lists to be memorized on pronunciations, idioms, slang, and grammar.

During interviews conducted for this project, two respondents employed with different large organizations shared the complete set of materials received during their language training. Each of these packages comprised an inch-thick set of black-and-white photocopied materials, spiral bound or stapled with clip art graphics. Most documents contain no copyright or author information with the exception of one booklet that is published by a specific global human resource organization and another that contains the name of the organization and the word "confidential" at the bottom of each page. Ironically, the materials themselves contain "Indianisms," such as the phrases "pronounce a word rightly" or "how the meaning would differ when one stresses on a particular word would be covered later." Densely packed pages in ten-point font cover topics such as "Essentials of Grammar," "Consonant Sounds," "Diphthongs," "Intonation," "Fluency, Pacing and Word Groups," "Speaking to Be Understood," "Comprehending Diverse Accents," and "Indianisms and Common Errors in Speech." Accompanying these training materials are assessment sheets used to measure and quantify progress. These sheets contain detailed measures with scores attached to them. Measures include items such as "should not have regional influence," "should have a neutral accent," "should have appropriate rate of speech," and "should enunciate all words correctly." Overall, the low-tech look and feel of the materials contrasts dramatically with their grandiose titles such as *Certificate in Customer Service.*

In these materials, three types of "Indianisms" that need to be avoided at all costs are identified: using typical English-Indian expressions, mixing English with regional languages, and translating from a regional language. Indians are characterized as being unnecessarily verbose, speaking at twice the universally accepted rate of speech, having a formal, written style of verbal communication, and frequently using politically incorrect or gender-insensitive terms. In addition, certain sounds are said to pose particular challenges for Indians, and these can "bring about a regional influence if not applied in the right manner." To this end, one manual provides detailed instructions on how to correctly pronounce various sounds, with a diagram of the mouth and arrows showing the correct position of the tongue, roof of mouth, teeth, and lips. In the accompanying text, it is noted that "the TH sound is often the hardest consonant for many non-native English speakers to learn. Practice putting your tongue very lightly against the back of your top teeth and blowing. The air should flow freely... You should be able to prolong it for 2 seconds. Your tongue can be between your upper and lower front teeth but should not stick out beyond your teeth or your tongue can be behind your top teeth."

Overall, the scope of language, communication, and culture training for customer service agents is mind-boggling. Their training materials contain pages of words that are phonetically spelled to capture various American, British, and Australian accents as well as detailed instructions on how to correct "Indianisms." Reviewing these materials, it is difficult to imagine that anyone could master the contents in a matter of weeks. The very scope of the training required suggests that rather than bridging the gap between ideal and possessed skills, training actually serves to highlight the vast and insurmountable gap between Western ideals and Indian workers.

The Western Neutral

Language training and accent neutralization is justified in training manuals as necessary to convert various ways of speaking English in India into a single, universally understood accent. This notion of global equality and interconnectedness pervades training materials,[16] where it is noted that "we live in a multicultural environment where we are required to interact with individuals and organizations from different cultural backgrounds. Therefore, it has become necessary that every individual and organization become aware of cross-cultural differences and their impact on their interactions." The global economy is said to create new opportunities as well as new responsibilities for workers. As stated in the manual, "[O]ur world is better connected today than it ever was. People from diverse cultures are interacting more than ever before. This necessitates that every individual and his/her culture is recognized and respected... We need to adopt a form of language that does not hurt the sentiments of any social group or imply any form of stereotyping." The rhetoric of respect for all cultures slips frequently, however, into a valorization of some. For example, frequent mention throughout the training materials are made to "global" or "neutral" English. Alongside this, however, there is a clear hierarchy between Indian versus American or British uses of English. In one training manual, it is noted that "an accent is never 'good' or 'bad'; it is different from others." Yet, at the same time, detailed practice exercises are provided to correct Indian English, which is equated with poor grammar. A table lists phrases under the title "wrong usage" on the left and "right usage" on the right. On the left, there are phrases such as "Even I do see" or "Can I suggest you something." Under the correct column, these same phrases appear "corrected" as "I see that" or "May I make a suggestion."

Not all non-neutral accents are deficient; certain diversities are valorized in the training materials. For example, one package contains separate detailed sections on American, British, and Australian accents. Detailed audio exercises are referred to, so trainees can learn about the different accents. Alongside the rhetoric that "Indianisms" undermine the ideal of universal comprehension possible through global English, learners are provided with detailed lists of "Americanisms" and "Britishisms" and are expected to memorize these. In one chapter learners are given a passage in Indian-English that they are asked to correct. The passage reads: "I am being happy due to the fact that my marriage is fixed with nice, foreign-returned boy also from Thakurpur. My brother is always pulling my legs because of that! I am also being excited because my all friends will be joining me in this happy occasion." The content of the passage is noteworthy—arranged marriage—and no doubt is chosen to provide a forum for discussion of distinctions between Indian and Western approaches to relationships during face-to-face training sessions. Another section contains pages of "British Slang" with terms such as *ace, barmy, bung, duff, kip, punter, suss,* which appear under the heading "Learning." A similar activity involves learning to understand an audio passage in Australian slang. In contrast to the passage about arranged marriages, the exercise about Australian English is about adventure and entrepreneurism: "A mate told me a bloke could make big bickies in Sydney. So I made for the big smokes flat chat to have a go at trying my bizzo there. Turns out I was such a galah. I reckon I should have had a chinwag with someone who could give me some good guts before I left." While the sections on "Indianisms" have exercises for the students to correct and achieve the neutrality needed for global understanding, the sections on Western slang are situated within subheadings such as "Appreciating Western Culture." In this way, training materials are engaged in "language trafficking,"[17] which translates into the spread of certain types of English across the world. The following respondent explains his interpretation of a neutral accent:

> In India, we speak English in a different [manner], and in the States, it is in a different way. [Interviewer: So they want you to learn—] A neutral accent. [Interviewer: What does that mean?] Neutral. Means they can understand what we tell. Like [for example] "schedule"—they say *sked*ule... And the American accent you have more *r*'s rolling, there's a stress on the *r*'s. So it's "sem-eye-conductor," it's not "se-me-conductor"... You're not supposed to speak anything except English, except American English.

The focus on developing "neutral" but Western accents suggests a confluence between capitalist and nationalist goals. Indian labor is constructed as a flexible and malleable commodity; accent neutralization serves to transform this human resource into one that can best meet client needs. The "neutral," however, contains a significant regional bias that implicitly identifies American, British, or Australian English as legitimate and Indian English as illegitimate.

Difference and Deficiency

Complex systems of language training are overtly designed to promote worker and customer understanding, but, in doing so, they also construct Indians as different from Westerners. In addition, authentic English speakers are those whom American, Australian, and British clients can understand and relate to. The relationship between skill and language is mediated by the location of workers and customers within national contexts and these contexts are defined through colonial pasts. The nationally oriented definition of skill has been cogently documented through studies that provide comparative analyses of Western and Indian workers. Selma Sonntag, for example, analyzes the job requirements of workers in a call center with offices in India, Canada, and Europe. Rather than universal requirements for similar jobs in different countries, European workers are required to possess strong business-writing skills and the ability to use English as a second language. Indian workers need to have exceptional English-language communication skills. Implicit is the assumption that Indians with exceptional English-language skills have equivalent abilities as English as a second language speakers in Europe.[18] In another study, Laurie Cohen and Amal El-Sawad report on the experiences of U.K. customer service representatives working in conjunction with agents in Mumbai employed by the same company. Their study reveals that "U.K. respondents expressed their unease not only with what they saw are some of their Indian colleagues' excessive desire to perfect their English, but with the results of these efforts, described by some as 'strange' and 'artificial'... UK staff spoke of these behaviors as disturbing because they were at once very familiar, and at the same time exotic and different."[19]

These responses from colleagues and employers in the West suggest that the relationship between language and skill is much more complex than the training provided on diction and rate of speech would suggest. While some call center workers in India see English language as a skill, many recognize that their legitimacy depends on much more than how they form their sentences. Two distinct discourses prevail in workers' discussions of their language: discourses of language as embodied knowledge and discourses of language as acquired skill. In general, the workers who are convent educated and from urban areas talk about English-language abilities as embodied traits, while others construct language as a skill. One convent-educated worker reflects:

> Like, no matter how much you train somebody. Now some of the people I'm not lying to you, and I meant it literally when I say they have grammar issues. You have to teach them how to speak proper English first... forget an accent or forget pronunciation. You need to get your *the*'s and *a*'s in position to speak well. And that I thought was a major issue that nobody really dealt with. If I was really recruiting somebody, I'd first pick somebody who knew how to speak good English... to speak good English, that is something that you have to teach somebody while in school. Not over six weeks of training. You can't rectify grammar issues or mother tongue influence. This is a very common problem I've seen with most Mahrashtran people I've seen work in BPOs. No matter how much they say that thing is always there, that thing is always there in their pronunciations.

Other workers with more limited class resources reject this construction of language as difficult to acquire. They report that Indians are malleable and trainable, and that language skills can be easily learned through successful training programs. In their view, training successes are widely celebrated and their success stories form a part of the motivational material used in training programs. A first-year university student who was simultaneously working at a call center recounts the benefits of the training he received: "I would say it's actually helping me to speak better in my normal life itself. Because I mean that is the proper mannerism of talking. After being with this organization I would say I've learned how to speak normally with people in my life as well. That's the proper way of speaking." A trainer shares a similar experience on the transformational potential of training:

> There was a workshop on speaking abilities. There was one female who came from some remote part of India and she was not very good in speaking English, so she was put in the back-office work, the non-voice part. She was doing very well there because she was intelligent, but she was not really able to confidently speak. So there was a workshop designed for her and some more people like her, and after that, she had shown a lot of improvement and she was taken for a voice process, which was a big achievement for her, and for the company.

To "sound right," all workers undergo training during which they are placed, and place one another, within class and regional hierarchies. Indeed, constructions of English as skill or trait are claims of legitimacy, and in this sense part of the authenticity work that workers do as part of their jobs.

Permanently Deficient Workers

Managers, trainers, and workers themselves note that not all workers can be trained to speak in neutral accents. The most "strange" and "artificial" workers are those deemed to have non-neutralizable accents. Implicit is the construction of appropriate and inappropriate Indian workers' communication skills: those that can be easily "neutralized" versus those that cannot. In the context of India's colonial history, language is intimately tied to issues of region and class. As discussed earlier in this chapter, English in India was both the language of the colonial administration and the language of the indigenous elite.[20] This privileged position of English continues to dominate contemporary India. As John observes, "good English and superior class are not just mutually complementary in India but also mutually compulsory... the default social category of the English speaker in India is the brahmanical elite and the "power" sects, all of whom would at some stage have studied in missionary schools... This could be seen as a colonial legacy. Knowing of English was for a long time linked to decent social status and good behavior."[21]

It is significant, in this context, that South Indian and rural accents are consistently constructed among customer service workers as the most problematic. One worker summarizes that "voice and accent training [is] mainly about removing people's South Indian accents." Another notes that "there were people who were coming from the local medium—like Marathi medium schools and all—they couldn't speak, and they couldn't handle the process at the same point of time. For them it was even worse, because if they tried to get the pronunciation right, they messed up on the process, they forget what they are supposed to do next." Hierarchies are enacted through training in a context where accent is not just a signifier of education or geographical location but, most important, a signifier of class. Accent differences are expressed by workers in terms of class hierarchies. One woman talked about how surprised she was to find people from "different strata" working alongside her at the call center. She described one of her colleagues as "uneducated" with significant "language problems" and went on to say that this person "lived in a place that was like a slum. There were times that I felt like telling her that 'some maid servants I've had are far more attractive than you are.' And 'they have more manners than you, and they are more soft spoken than you are.'"

Accent also relates to the colonial heritage of educational hierarchies set up during British rule in India where English-medium convent schools were established to train the local elite.[22] Convent school graduates are normatively preferred for call center work, as noted by one participant in the study: "When you're a convent-educated girl and you show relevant experience, they hire you." Language serves as a stratification device through which class and regional hierarchies between workers are enacted. While the focus on the removal of "Indianisms" suggests that neutral accents are those spoken by the convent-educated, Indian elite, even workers from convent backgrounds are assumed to require remedial corrections in their way of speaking. For example, one woman with a convent education was unable to get a job at a call center despite several attempts. She attributes her failure to her refusal to dress in revealing Western clothing, although she says that recruiters provide no feedback to unsuccessful candidates. Giving up on finding employment at a call center, she notes that, "this kind of criticism is not for good... Well, it hurts me a lot. Then I would have an inferiority complex, which I don't want to have."

In fact, training materials refer noncategorically to all Indians as "non-native speakers of the English language... Indians tend to be very verbose both while speaking and writing in English, as compared to the casual speech patterns of native speakers of English."[23] This non-native status is enacted not only through training but also in the daily encounters between workers and customers. However, it is the workers' responsibility to maintain the linguistic hierarchy between themselves and their customers. One worker discusses the repercussions of challenging this linguistic hierarchy:

> Brits, they are so sarcastic that, you know, they'll eat you psychologically, slowly, slowly, and God forbid, if anybody tries to be oversmart and uses a jargon, he is gone because English is *their* language. And once they feel he is trying to be oversmart he is gone... Once I just used the word "imperative," I mean even now I use it because I know the meaning, and I feel that it is a normal word. But my trainer warned me once, don't use this word. But then I'm so habituated with this word that it came in naturally. So I used this word and then he started using a totally different level of English. He was talking normally and then he started—"I was trying to contemplate this bill," and I couldn't comprehend it.

In these interactions over the phone, using complex words is equated with sounding "fake" and failing to be understood. Understanding, being understood, and coming across as genuine are preconditions for the enactment of hierarchy between customers and workers. Language training thus aims not only to develop a "neutral" accent but also to communicate work norms and the culture of deference and servitude. In training materials, one section entitled "Building Rapport" illustrates the emphasis on deference and servitude by outlining the EAR method: This method involves empathizing with the customer, apologizing for the problem and accepting responsibility in order to help the client. In this material, the EAR method clearly outlines a distinction drawn between "empathy" and "sympathy" by noting: "Remember you are part of a system of service. The customers are out there on their own, in chaos and emotional turbulence. It is important to be sensitive to the customer's emotional state and build a precise skill to deal with it. Empathy is not sympathy, don't cry with, but take care of the customer."

Being part of a system of service involves responding with empathy and speaking in a particular way. This is true for customer service workers everywhere in the world. In transnational service work, however, the requirement for deference maps onto racially defined language hierarchies. Training defines Indians as deficient not only in language but also in culture. Traditions such as arranged marriage are used to demonstrate "Indianisms," while Westernisms are explained via stories of entrepreneurism and adventure (such as making bickies in Sydney). In the training process, attention is drawn to the link between language and culture. For example, in a section from one of the training materials on "barriers to fluency," it is noted that "an individual who belongs to a conservative society might not be expressive or vocal about his or her thoughts; or an individual who has not been exposed to an English-speaking environment, in spite of being excellent in written English, would be unable to string his thoughts in English comfortably." In this case, the links between English exposure, a conservative society, and expressiveness serve to entrench the distinctions between the "modern" and the "traditional."

Indeed there is a confluence of language use, work norms, and culture in transnational service work. During training and recruitment, workers are simultaneously assessed for language use and outlook. As part of the process, the topic of arranged marriages seems to be almost universally used during recruitment and training exercises. One worker reports that he was asked to speak into a recorder on the topic of "love marriage versus arranged marriage" and was later given feedback on his rate of speech, accent, and tone. In regard to the importance of the topic "marriage" in recruitment and training, a manager reports,

> We ask most of the interviewees, "What do you think is the difference in live-in relationship and married life?" That makes a big difference because you also speak about the American culture and the Indian culture. And the

> person who can speak about it, we can say, OK, this guy can do [the job] because he can speak about American culture also. But most of the guys, for them, they never saw a live-in relationship. [Interviewer: Why would this affect the ability to do the job?] Because at the end of the day, we want someone to understand them. That really makes a big difference on calls. You should understand what the person is going through.

Carol Upadhya observes that training programs and work cultures in Indian IT firms establish a juxtaposition between pluralistic Western cultures based on individualism, materialism, and personal achievement and Indian traditional family cultures based on authoritarianism, traditionalism, and religiosity.[24] This hierarchical distinction between the progressive and the backward runs through interviews with Indian customer service workers as they describe their ways and places of work. Workers note that not only do they need to sound a particular way but they are also often required to become particular kinds of people:

> I was very shy when I just joined my new organization... And saw that, you know, how people didn't agree with people who were shy. How they make you nervous and, you know, when you speak, you were asked to do projects and, you know, you were asked to stand in front of so many people and everybody is judging you... So I did see that you have to be a certain way... somebody who comes across to be very bold. I don't know what to say, wouldn't say provocative behavior, but I did see a lot of girls who were that and they'd manage to, you know.

> I had to change, I realized that if I was going to be shy, people are just going to eat me raw. They are going to have fun at my expense, and I had to, I was left with no choice but to change. It was kind of realizing about what people are all about. You're respected if you're a certain way, you're not respected if you're a certain way. People always thought that I was this dumb girl who had everything but it's not like that. People think I don't have problems at work, even today where I work, "What problems can you have, you wear good clothes, you look good, you come live in a good society," but they don't realize ever since I've come here, I'm a totally different person. Ever since I've come to this industry, I'm a totally different person.

In the context of transnational call center work, becoming a totally "different" person involves emulating the traits, outlooks, and ways of being of Western clients, as will be explored in Chapter 4. Just as discourses of deficiency structure language training, these discourses also construct workers as needing control and structure to clone Western standards of professionalism. Stuart Hall has explored the ways in which the notion of the "West" functions as a mechanism through which societies can be classified and, more important, ranked. In this manner, he notes that the "West is a historical not a geographical construct... [and refers to] a society that is developed, industrialized, urbanized, capitalist, secular and modern."[25] In fact, part of the aesthetic labor of working in transnational call centers involves becoming Westernized and, in return, defining local cultures, languages, and customs as backward and incorrect. Through training and work process, the difference between India and the West is enacted to allow Indians to be "understood" by Westerners. Overall, this difference is constructed not only in terms of language and culture but also in terms of nationalist policies and histories as explored in the next chapter.

3

Hate Nationalism and the Outsourcing Backlash

While telephone lines are crystal clear, call center workers are at the front line of the static-filled cross-connections arising from the opposing rhetoric of global capitalism and nationalism. Free trade agreements idealize the unfettered transfer of capital according to the demands of the market. At the same time, national governments are elected on platforms that promise access to jobs for residents.[1] The jousting between protectionism and free trade occurs on a daily basis on the calls between Indian customer service agents in India and customers in the West. This chapter explores the ways in which, through these conversations, national interests are defined and nationalisms exercised.

Abandoning Locational Masking

Over the past decade, there seems to have been a remarkable shift in management policies and workplace practices within call centers in India. Customer service agents interviewed in the early 2000s were required to go to extreme lengths to mask their physical locations in India. By 2005, almost all the customer service agents interviewed reported that they were allowed to openly acknowledge their location in India to Western clients over the phone. One worker describes this shift by noting that "initially, we had this company policy where you are not supposed to tell. Like even if the customer asks, 'Are you from India?' we were supposed to tell that it is our company policy that we are not supposed to tell which part of the world we belong to. We just represent this company and we just provide the support. Well, somewhere in between again the company change its policy that if the customer asks where you are, you can go ahead and tell them that you are located in India." Ironically, this open revelation about the location of work occurred right after the heavily publicized "outsourcing backlash" that gained momentum in 2003 and 2004 in the United States, United Kingdom, Canada, and Australia. I argue that this dramatic change in policy can be understood in the context of the shifting debates on outsourcing within the West. The outsourcing backlash was, in fact, a mechanism for nation building. As a result, it solidified the distance between Westerners and Indians—the latter constructed as outsiders and dishonest strangers who are far away from the source of power and capital.

The expansive training systems described in Chapter 2 are justified in terms of the need for Indians not only to learn to speak to Westerners but also to make customers feel as though they could be talking to someone from their own local settings. In the early 2000s, workers faced severe penalties if they revealed their geographical location in India. They were trained in locational masking by being required to follow scripted responses designed to evade customer queries on the location of worksites. As noted in a news report entitled "Hi, I'm in Bangalore (but I Can't Say So)" one worker introduces herself as "Susan Sanders from Chicago" and recounts a "fictional American life, with parents Bob and Ann, brother Mark and a made-up business degree from the University of Illinois."[2] Winifred Poster's interviews with workers in 2002 and 2003 corroborate this view as she constructs a composite "Anil" based on her interviews:

> Anil has practiced a script, to be used for the looming question from customers: "Where are you calling from?" From experience, he knows he will be asked this question many times during his shift. He has been given a

> carefully prepared set of responses by his supervisor. Last week he was on a campaign that required him to say he was in the Miami office of the client firm. This week, he needs to be more circuitous: "First, we say we are calling from an 'outbound call center.' If they ask again, then we say we are 'in Asia.' If they ask again, then we change the subject." Under the worst scenario, if the customer becomes hostile very early in the call, then he has a fallback strategy: to say he is an Indian immigrant living in the United States.[3]

Workers interviewed in the early stages of data collection for this book (2002–2004) recount similar ways in which they are required to overtly lie to customers. One agent recounts the instructions he was given: "Don't tell them that we are in India. They totally avoid it... because the customers are in Simonton in Texas. That's where our main office [is]. So we tell them we are in Texas. So, sometimes people say 'Where are you?' Because of the accent... obviously a little bit difference will still stay. Even after the training and stuff. They still understand. This is not a typical American. So they will ask you... 'Where are you?' [and I answered], 'right now I am in U.S. I am in Simonton.'"

Masking location goes hand in hand with masking identities. Workers were assigned fictional names—and these were more than pseudonyms because workers were required to use these names not only on calls but in all interactions in the workplace. In some organizations, "naming ceremonies" were held to confer assigned Western names.[4] Indian organizations are often required to sign nondisclosure agreements with their Western clients. They develop protocols to ensure that customers are not made aware of their location in India. Such requirements enact a form of "production fetishism"[5] where the exact nature of the transnational flows of labor and capital that are involved in the production of a product or service are masked. As summarized in a news report in the early 2000s, "the point of this pretense is to convince Americans who dial toll-free numbers that the person on the other end of the line works right nearby—not 8,300 miles away, in a country where static-free calls used to be a novelty."[6]

Although widespread in the early 2000s, locational masking was not always successful. Many respondents acknowledged that their efforts to conceal their location frequently failed and generated customer anger. One worker reported: "One day a person went, you know, 'I don't want to speak to you. You have broken English. Please give me someone American'."

When asked by clients where he was, one worker specifically described his approach and the negative reactions he received from customers:

> Where are you? So we try to just come out of it, just say, "This is Warranty Service." I know what he's asking about, but still I need to say this. "No, I want to know where you are located." "This is the warranty service center, and we are not allowed to disclose our location." We need to say very frankly. "Why some secret is happening over there? I know you are in Bangalore, I know you are in Mumbai." Things like that they used to say. Sometimes you need to give false statements. Once a customer called over here, he said in Hindi "shukriya" [thank you]. I was not very used to it, I was still very new to the phone. So I said "okay thank you." He said, yea, "you know Hindi man, I said 'shukriya' and you said 'thank-you.' Are you in India?", so again I have to say, "No sir, I've never been to India."

Locational masking sometimes required workers to construct themselves as deficient or unknowing. One agent who avidly follows politics recounts the following incident when a U.S. customer of Indian origin knew that he was likely talking to someone in India. He asked: "'How is your relationship with Pakistan going?' And things like, 'has Kashmir improved?' You can't say anything. I told the . . . person, 'I'm not much involved in the politics. I don't read newspapers.'"

Despite being so strongly entrenched, by 2005, management commitment to location masking had disappeared. This was presented to workers as a change of policy; the decision to abandon locational masking was seen to have been made in faraway headquarters.[7] Although workers did not receive any formal explanation for this shift, they made sense of it by noting the impossibility of concealing the geographical distance between India and the West. As one worker explains, "People sometimes get annoyed when they find out that they are calling India, especially when we are told not to say we are in India. No matter how good our accent is, they come to know. Like how we come to know, say we have a foreigner who speaks very good Hindi, grammatically correct, but he's still not an Indian, we do come to know. Same way they will come to know. No matter how much we try to hide it."

Instead of scripted responses to evade questions related to their location, agents were asked to attempt to appease callers, and if this strategy failed, transfer their calls to call centers in the West: "They used to ask us to transfer the call, but we used to always say is whatever they are going to tell you is the same as we tell you, the only thing is that we are in India and they are in the U.S. Then it's left up to them to make the choice whether they want to speak to us or to a [agent] in U.S. [Are you penalized for transferring calls?] No, we are not...[You don't try to convince them to continue to talk to you?] No, because we had to go ahead and transfer the calls because it's again the customer who is king, so whatever they want." In a few cases, even the use of pseudonyms was discontinued; as one worker interviewed in 2006 reports, "If the person is asking 'where are you?' we can tell them we are in India and we are not provided with any kind of pseudonym. We used to speak our original names. And we used to tell that 'I am in India and my name is this.' They wanted transparency between the customer and the agent whom they are talking to."

This dramatic shift from locational masking to the open acknowledgment of work in India is particularly surprising in the context of Western debates on outsourcing occurring between 2003 and 2004. During that time, there was a strong public backlash, which was supported by unions, newspapers, and politicians and emerged in striking symphony in Canada, United States, United Kingdom, and Australia. In this context, one would have expected attempts to conceal the outsourcing of work to intensify rather than disappear. As I argue below, however, public backlash largely failed to curb capitalist interests and halt offshoring. In this context, the acknowledgment of the distant, faraway location of Indian customer service workers served important purposes for the everyday expression of Western nationalism.

Expressions of nationalism take three forms in relation to Indian customer service work.[8] First, it is the creation of the boundaries within which nation-states exist. Rather than a focus on a physical territory, this takes the form of the assignment of citizenship to jobs, whereby national ownership is attributed to and claimed to inherently reside in certain jobs. In this manner, jobs are personified and bestowed a citizenship. Second, it is the construction of those outside the nation as strange and different. Finally, it is the rhetoric of fear whereby strangers are seen as threatening to the nation and objects of hate. These expressions of nationalism are manifest in different but overlapping ways in the United States, United Kingdom, Canada, and Australia.[9]

Expressions of Nationalism: Revenge of the Colonies

The 2004 U.S. election is widely acknowledged as a watershed moment for the Indian IT and customer service work sectors. In the weeks leading up to the election, candidate John Kerry made a sweeping promise, saying, "When I am President, and with your help, we're going to repeal every benefit, every loophole, every reward that entices any... company or CEO to take the money and the jobs overseas and stick the American people with the bill."[10] Kerry's speech seemed to open a floodgate of public expression, media analysis, and political jousting. It also added fuel to a debate that was clearly already occurring in many circles. In high-profile forums such as Lou Dobb's "Exporting America" series, business leaders were targeted with public shamings for allegedly exporting "American jobs" to overseas locations. In another scandalous revelation, it was found that the customer service activities for a New Jersey food stamp program, which was operated by a private contractor, had been shifted to India. A community leader is reported as saying, "it is unconscionable to send state-funded jobs overseas in the face of the staggering number of unemployed New Yorkers."[11] Similar trends were occurring in Australia, where customers responded with outrage to the publicity about Indian workers dealing with Coles Myer's credit inquiries. One customer notes, "I was particularly annoyed because it's a Myer. It's a local institution. If I was ringing to ask about my Visa I wouldn't mind. Myer is complicit in a subterfuge and I will be giving up my card."[12] In the United Kingdom, in 2003, the Communications Workers Union launched a high-profile campaign focusing on British Telecom (BT)'s decision to outsource work to India. The union held BT responsible for exporting "British jobs."[13]

Much of the discussion of outsourcing occurring in the West has been in relation to "human interest stories" profiling individuals experiencing job loss. A *New York Times* Father's Day editorial characterizes outsourcing as "a form of intimate, familial robbery."[14] Michael Palm notes that "the most resonant human interest stories followed workers who had lost their manufacturing jobs during one or another recession, then managed to finance their own reskilling, and now are losing the very white-collar jobs that they had fashioned themselves to qualify for. The plights of these versatile and resilient workers are a central concern for anyone sympathetic to labor in the US."[15]

Discourses of nationalism are rampant in these outsourcing debates. The primary "citizens" at the center of the discussions are the jobs that are infused with national character. In direct contrast to the free trade language of mobility and international exchange, jobs are claimed as citizens of particular Western nations. In the United States, this protective embodiment of jobs was enacted through the introduction of over two hundred bills in state legislatures since 2004 such as the Commission on American Jobs Act and the Keeping American Jobs at Home Act.[16] After much publicity, only a half dozen of these bills became law. These were the most innocuous of the proposals, requiring only the disclosure or collection of information on the impacts of outsourcing. The strongest anti-outsourcing legislation was passed in New Jersey with Bill 494, which prohibits state contract work from being performed outside the United States. As summarized in the 2007 National Foundation for American Policy Brief, "many state efforts to restrict global sourcing are likely unconstitutional or violate trade agreements."[17] Attempts to quantify the actual numbers of jobs saved or lost in the West were also mired in controversy, and research showed no clear evidence that trade protection could actually prevent job loss.[18] Research findings from large projects such as the Global Call Center Project reveal that there is little evidence that large numbers of jobs are being shifted from North America and Europe to emerging markets. Rather, India and the Philippines have absorbed newly created jobs and the call center sector has experienced faster growth in these countries than in the West. In fact, the percentage of the workforce employed as call center workers has remained stable in Western countries. As Rosemary Batt and her colleagues summarize, "off-shore call center services represent a much smaller proportion of global activity than media accounts have suggested."[19]

Despite the lack of empirical support and the failure of policy outcomes, this largely theatrical outcry against outsourcing continues to pervade U.S. politics. In response to the economic crisis of 2009, President Obama is quoted as saying that "it's time to finally slash the tax breaks for companies that ship our jobs overseas and give those tax breaks to companies that create jobs in the United States of America.... [About the current tax system:] It's a tax code that says you should pay lower taxes if you create a job in Bangalore, India, than if you create one in Buffalo, USA."

Supported by such speeches, discussions of outsourcing in the West involve bestowing citizenship to jobs. From this perspective, protecting these

"American jobs" or "British jobs" is necessary to protect the nation. Such everyday nationalism is exercised by Western politicians, media, and the public through expressions of anti-outsourcing. Poster argues that "turning outsourcing into a symbol of nationalism helps politicians obscure and evade larger issues like de-industrialization, the withering state support for workers, sky-rocketing health costs, and declining real wages."[20] The vociferous political speech making and public discussion around the anti-outsourcing bills essentially serve as a platform for the display of American nationalism rather than for the revision of economic policy.

Accompanying the definition of the citizenship of the jobs as "American," "Canadian," "British," or "Australian," is the construction of Indians as threatening strangers. These discourses of "stranger danger"[21] are most vividly illustrated in the Communications Workers Union 2003 campaign called "Pink Elephant—Stop the Job Stampede to India." The campaign

Pink Elephant Campaign. Courtesy of Communications Workers' Union

began with a cross-country march originating in a small Scottish highland village (John O'Groats). India was represented by Pinky, a huge inflatable pink elephant: "Pinky appears variously on campaign material as the villain of the piece: he is carrying suitcases and heading for India; kicking over boxes bearing the words 'UK jobs,' 'UK economy,' 'UK customers,' 'UK revenues.' In one poster... Pinky is seen answering a call while sitting in front of an Eastern cityscape from a tearful white woman who has lost her call center job and wants to speak on the telephone to the job center."[22] In another image, Pinky is shown following a signpost that reads "BT call centre: 4,200 miles."

Much is conveyed through the image of the elephant: India's size, traditionalism, and non-Western religiosity.[23] This elephant, however, is distinctive in that it is pink, and therefore unreal, unknown, strange, and alien. Sara Ahmed argues that "[aliens] allow the demarcation of spaces of belonging; by coming too close to home, they establish the very necessity of policing the borders of knowable and sustainable terrains... it allows us to share a fantasy that, in the co-presence of strange and alien bodies, we will prevail."[24] With the growing feasibility of the outsourcing of service work comes the increased need to depict India and Indians as strange outsiders and job pirates.

The rhetoric of fear in relation to India and Indians is also rampant. In a speech introducing a bill on outsourcing in the Oregon legislature, Senator Ron Wyden notes, "an offshoring tsunami is bearing down on workers in the information technology and services sector."[25] A journalist similarly argues that "over the next decade, offshoring will knock millions of white-collar Americans and Europeans out of work, blowing a hole in the middle class from Los Angeles to London, from Boston to Berlin, from Toledo to Tokyo, from Austin to Amsterdam... call it the revenge of the colonies, but any developing country with lots of English speakers and good Internet links is now a prime jobs magnet."[26]

Discourses portraying Indians as thieves also continue to be actively reproduced through intermittent reports of fraud or customer abuse in relation to outsourced customer service work.[27] Customer anger about telemarketing is seamlessly funneled into expressions of anti-outsourcing nationalism. On January 19, 2011, *The Toronto Star* reported that a major Canadian telecommunications company, Bell Canada, had been fined $1.3 million by the federal regulator that had received ten thousand customer complaints about aggressive and abusive telemarketing calls made by Bell employees. The reporter notes that some telemarketing is contracted out rather than performed in-house and that organizations have little control over the labor processes of subcontractors. In passing, it is mentioned that some contactors are located in India. Within twelve hours, 163 comments had been posted in response to this article, referring to Indians as "crude," "cheap labor," and "people who do not speak English." Commentators lamented the days when Bell Canada was a Canadian icon and characterized outsourcing as having destroyed the company. One person notes that outsourcing should be added to the Criminal Code.[28] Another example of such a response occurred in April 2010 when I was interviewed on a Canadian radio show. I shared worker experiences of customer abuse and aggression. A comment posted in response to the article reads, "I abuse them every chance I get. They do not speak English, but a language only they can understand. They lie through their teeth and always have an 'attitude'. They are what I call sub-human and I HATE them."[29] Poster draws parallels between these efforts in fearmongering and the Bush rhetoric on the "war on terror." She notes that "the rhetoric of empire is apparent in Indian call centers—not through an explicit language of racial superiority—but through the mediating language of 'terror,' and the denigration of South Asian, Middle Eastern, and Muslim identities. Globalized service work is providing a new forum for everyday citizens to articulate this kind of nationalized rhetoric."[30]

Most significantly, such a focus on thieving Indians allows customers to express their frustrations at the rising levels of precarious employment and falling standards of living within the West. State anti-outsourcing rhetoric legitimizes customers' use of their on-the-phone interactions with Indian customer service workers as sites where they can express anger and frustration about local and global economic trends.[31]

Indian customer service agents are not passive bystanders in these expressions of Western nationalism. One worker recounts his response to an abusive caller:

> Some people are very unhappy about the whole idea of the things being outsourced to India . . . [I say,] "in case you have any personal grudge with me, you could always hang up the call and call back. If you want me to assist [you], I would be very happy." It was a very simple and blunt statement . . . but

> I need to maintain my dignity, my Indian dignity as well...I remember a call coming in, everything was done...and he was barking at me that "you are in India." So my blunt reply was "How does it matter whether I was in Sri Lanka, Pakistan, or anywhere else?" I said, "I did your job, it's done on a toll-free number, what else are you looking for?" The call was recorded in Halifax, and the comment came from there that, yes, you should maintain your personal dignity as well.

The incident described above was a rare example of worker dissent. Most workers imagined such responses but attempted to diffuse customer anger through deference and apology. Their calls were monitored and customer feedback sought, which served to promote worker servitude on calls. During interviews, however, workers shared both their responses to customers and the answers they wished they could give. They discussed their experiences with customers as well as their imagined encounters around the anti-outsourcing backlash. These imagined encounters allowed workers to cope with the racism that now forms a growing component of their jobs.

Imagined and Experienced Encounters

Although the proposed 2004 bill to "Disclose location of call center upon request" did not pass in California, management strategy in Indian call centers shifted in this direction. Despite the limited success of the outsourcing backlash, outsourcing became a widely discussed social issue with arguments made not only against the trend but also in its support. The U.K. government, for example, noted that outsourcing had generated a net benefit for Britain by maximizing profits and lowering consumer costs. Similarly, the 2007 U.S. Bureau of Labor Statistics professed that only 2 percent of the recent layoffs within companies of more than fifty employees cited outsourcing as a factor.[32] These debates, many of which failed to address the concerns of individual workers' holding precarious jobs in numerous sectors, did provide the opportunity for a focused, active discussion on whether Western national interests were served or undermined by outsourcing—an issue on which politicians as well as the general public (including customers) had a variety of opinions.

While these debates raged in the West, Indian customer service agents were at the forefront of these expressions of nationalism. As management strategy shifted away from locational masking, dealing with racism became an even more predominant part of their jobs. No longer allowed to pretend that they were located in the West, agents satisfied the need for the public in the West to voice their anger. Several workers reported that the failure to disclose their location in India was deemed a "fatal error" for which they could be fired instantaneously.

Constructed as strangers, outsiders, and thieves, Indian customer service workers report several strategies for dealing with the constant everyday expressions of nationalism and racism that they encounter. One technique involves defining the work of dealing with customer anger as highly skilled work requiring a clear understanding of why customers are upset and how they can be appeased through empathy. In their imagined encounters with customers, agents empathize with customer anxieties around job loss. One worker, for example, shares his analysis of protectionism by noting, "What happened is, it was publicized and Bush didn't want outsourcing going on, so they all knew that jobs are being outsourced and their accounts are being dealt with in India, so they knew about it." Another worker justifies customer anger: "They may ask you, 'I bought a [product] and I should get support from an American, why should I get support from an Indian?'" Workers also legitimize security concerns: "They have a mindset that they are talking to Indians. They are out of the U.S. Why they are calling us? It might be a scam. It can be a scam."

Melissa Wright studies the ways in which discourses of nationality play a role in differentiating between more and less valuable workers. In her study of Asian and Mexican branches of an American multinational company, she shows how hierarchies among workers across national contexts are validated through their link to notions of skill, whereby American engineers claim their own skill (and the lack of others' skills) as a way of gaining status and resources.[33] In line with this, Indian workers construct their ability to deal with customer racism as a part of the skills required in their jobs; as one worker explains, "U.K. customers and U.S.A. customers, they really did not want to speak to Indians. Obviously being an Indian . . . we had to put [up with it]. . . . We have to give good service for the customer. That matters. Whether he is irate or he is abusing us. It really doesn't matter. We have taken this job. We have to do the job properly. That's what matters."

A second way that workers deal with anti-outsourcing anger is to draw attention to the locus of decision making in the West rather than in India. Workers refer to the economic benefits of outsourcing accrued to Western consumers. One worker imagines the following interaction with customers:

> There are people who would tell you, "I don't want to buy anything from people selling me overseas. If you want to sell me something, come to my country and sell me." And so you need to tell them... "I am not calling to cheat you or anything. We have 50,000 business clients in Australia itself... We are located in Australia itself. Even our customer service is in Australia. So it's only our sales department who has come here in India. And it is going to benefit your own Australian clients. Because if you buy something from there, you pay more. The only reason I am calling you from India, you are getting this cheap."

At the same time, there is considerable ambivalence on the economic discourses through which outsourcing is justified, and some workers are decidedly uncomfortable with the notion that they are "cheap labor." For example, one worker reflects: "They would be like 'Indian people, cheap people. Working for less than what we earn in a day.' And all that crap. And that would really hurt. I mean, they shouldn't have that thinking about us." Another worker imagines responding to customers with anger: "They have no right to tell us that 'you bloody Indians doing it' because one of your bloody people has given it to us. They find us more trainable, more intelligent, more adjustable, and more economic. But I won't say cheap. Cheap is a cheap word actually. More economic."[34]

A third, closely related way in which Indians respond to expressions of Western anti-outsourcing nationalism is by exercising nationalism themselves. A worker reflects on a call in which a successful resolution had been reached: "We've been given an alias... I've been given the name Nick... Maybe a problem which I know it will take one and a half hours to solve, and I solve it in twenty minutes. I'm very much happy and satisfied. Customer, he's also very happy. He... congratulates, 'Well done! You really helped me,' and then he asks you your name. If I give my own identity, I'm more satisfied. 'I'm [his name], I did the job.' [pause] I'm not Nick! I don't know who Nick is, then what's the use of giving my alias when *I'm* the one working, *I'm* solving the problem, *I'm* from India? ... [But] no, we cannot give my name."

Finally, Indians imagine responding to customer racism by raising issues of class and by specifically drawing attention to their middle-class status. If customers were better informed of their class status, they imagine that they would be treated with greater respect. Indian customer service representatives overtly and frequently refer to class differences between themselves (as highly educated and middle-class) and the Western public they serve. For example, one manager reports that his CEO often says that "an average American is uneducated." A worker similarly comments, "A kid in India will know more about mobiles than an adult in the U.K." This class difference is highlighted in training programs. A worker describes scenarios provided during their training to illustrate responses workers should expect from American customers:

> They don't know anything about computers.... If you say to them, just go to the start button, they will not be able to find the start button. "Where is the start button?"... And sometimes people are... talking about the troubleshooting steps, and they're not sitting in front of their computers. [They say] "I'm not able to see anything." And then we ask, "Are you sitting in front of your computer?" He said, "No, I'm not sitting in front of my computer." My God! One time [someone] called up and he said, "You sent me a coffee mug tray and it was broken, send me another one."... We asked our supervisor, was there any such scheme of sending in a coffee tray along with the [computer]?... Then [we realized] it was the CD drive! He used to put his coffee mug! We have so many examples like that. My God!

Many workers refer to the fact that while customers have little knowledge, they have high disposable incomes:

> There are a lot of old people also that are hard of hearing, and you have to talk to them like you're explaining to a little child, because a lot of them are not very good with mobile phone, and they don't even know what a SIM card is, and people say GOSH! Are Americans so dumb?, they don't even know what a SIM card is. Probably when mobile phones came to India, Indians were the same, a lot of people don't understand that they don't have patience to understand that. You have to explain to them like little children how to put the phone, how to put the SIM card together.

> They don't know anything about computers. They put the [CD] upside down... We ask, "OK, how are you putting it in? The shiny portion should be down."... Previously, before we started interacting with Americans, I

> basically had what I might refer to as [pause] it was in my mind, they are really good, they are really very intelligent, they have a lot of knowledge, nobody can beat the Americans. That was what my perception was. When I started handling calls, the type of questions they ask, I said, "Oh, it's bad. They only have money. They don't have brains."

In these ways, workers draw attention to the uneven development (which privileges national origin rather than education or intelligence) fostered by global capitalism.[35] One worker reports, "Because they ruled us, they think we're inferior." Another notes, "Some Americans, they call [and] say, 'I want to talk to an American.' Oh man, go on! You got an Indian and you are telling an Indian that you want to talk to an American!... Some of them, they really speak very very fast and that is a bit difficult... In any case, we have to handle the calls. We can't say that, 'you are an American, we can't talk to you.' Like they have the freedom to say anything, but we can't say anything." Through reinforcing the distinction between "us" and "them," Indians give value to their work. One worker wishes she could respond to customers' derogatory remarks: "They literally say, at times, that 'you bloody Indians don't know how to speak English. Can I speak to someone who can speak English.' We transfer the call, but they should not say that... 'Sir, I can speak many languages. Can you? Think about that. You don't have to humiliate anyone.'"

While workers imagine such responses, they do not confront customers on the phone and know that they could face severe penalties for challenging customers. As such, there remains an insurmountable gulf between their imagined encounters with their customers and their actual experiences on calls. Workers experience Western customers as irrational and violent, and respondents collectively provide hundreds of examples of customer aggression. They note that these angry responses from customers have intensified since the 2004 U.S. presidential election.[36] Arjun Appadurai argues that contemporary global capitalism is dominated by consumer fetishism, which is the illusion that the customer is the most important social actor in business arrangements. He notes that this is a "mask for the real seat of agency, which is not the consumer but the producer and the many forces that constitute production."[37] While Appadurai argues that consumers have limited control, the anonymity of phone service allows them to exercise considerable power. In the context of the hierarchy between Western customers and Indian service providers, this power is often expressed in the form of racism. One worker, interviewed for a news report, comments, "when some callers are unhappy with the service, their frustration often turns racist... they would say, 'This is why you should not handle our work. Indians are not good enough.'"[38] In the context of the outsourcing backlash, this racism is pointedly nationalist, and Indian call center workers are continually accused of personally "stealing" American jobs. One agent recounts: "Americans are not really happy outsourcing the job to India. Because I still remember a call from a very old guy, and after doing all the things possible to satisfy his needs, he made one statement, 'You know Vince, you did a great job, however, I hate you... because I hate all Indians. And my son is unemployed because of you, because the jobs are being outsourced to India.'" This discourse of "hate" runs through many workers' accounts of their work: "You get a lady... she used to work in a call center. She called up just to say that 'you people are just so scripted, and I hate you people and I hate you Indians just because of that.'" Ahmed characterizes hate as an "affective economy" that sticks "figures of 'hate' together, transforming them into a common threat... the bodies of others are hence transformed into 'the hated' through a discourse of pain. They are assumed to 'cause' injury to the ordinary white subject."[39] Customers, therefore, play an active role in defining global relations by seeking to sabotage attempts made by transnational corporations to shift the servicing of their needs to low-wage countries. They do this by expressing racist anger on the phone: "[Sometimes] the customer, the client, he knows everything. As soon as we pick up the phone, from there he himself, he or she himself or herself, says, 'My name is this, my [number] is this,... I'm fine today'... There are customers who say, 'I know you're from Delhi, or you're from India. I know the supervisor also. So don't fool around with me.'"

In these ways, hierarchies between workers and customers are continually enacted in transnational call center organizations. Customer superiority, which is already reified in the production process, is exercised via racist expression that serves nationalist interests. On one side, workers are closely monitored and easily identified through telephone and computer technologies. Their words are more closely and easily recorded than those of other workers in face-to-face service settings. In general, call center workers are aware that they can be easily traced by customers and that supervisors frequently listen to their calls. On the side of the customers calling in, there is little accountability because their responses remain largely anonymous and free from the normative requirements of public interactions as they are often calling from the privacy of their homes. Customer ethnocentricism can be freely exercised through consumer "choice" when customers prefer domestic products and judge services provided by foreigners as inferior.[40] This power differential, together with the information that work is located in India, leads to an augmentation of customer power. For example, one worker notes that "the moment they know you are from India, they directly say, 'I should not be telling this to you. FUCKING Indian.'" Customers freely express racialized stereotypes as reported by an agent: "Are you Indian? They'll give me as many bad languages they have: 'Don't talk to me. What you did on September 11th, World Trade Center'... There was a bomb blast in U.K... That day, not a single U.K. guy was talking with us. 'You did a bomb blast. Don't talk with us. Get lost.'" In almost all interviews, workers shared stories of harassment: "Many of the customers when they call, and you say the welcome phrase, they just ask one single [question]—'Am I calling India?' If you say yes, they just ask 'I want to talk to someone in the U.S., I don't want to talk to Indians,' and at that point of time, we have to tolerate and we cannot say anything because it is our job responsibility as well as it comes under our customer satisfaction... parameters."

Ahmed asks, "What effects do such encounters have on the bodies of others who become transformed into objects of hate?"[41] Perhaps the most insidious aspects about discourses of hate are the ways in which the inherent hierarchies are normalized. For customer service workers, dealing with racism is constructed through training, performance measures, and on-the-job feedback as a normal part of their jobs. Workers come to expect customer racism and are trained to manage their emotional reactions to abuse. More than just a part of customer service work, however, normalizing customer racism sanctions the expression of everyday anti-outsourcing anger on the part of Western customers. Transnational customer service forms a legitimate forum for public expression of the need to protect "American," "Canadian," "Australian," or "British" jobs. Violence on calls is socially productive and serves to build community within the West.[42] Transnational customer service interactions provide a concrete target upon which customers in the West can express their anxiety not only about offshoring but also about globalization in general. Through their anti-outsourcing nationalism, customers engage in a "process of we-making"[43] where they define themselves as legitimate job holders and Indians as job thieves. Whether related to their ethnic hatred or their anxieties about globalization, agents in India often experience callers as shockingly aggressive. Yet in raising issues of class, skill, and the economic reasoning behind subcontracting, customer service agents construct Westerners as protectionist, parochial, and unreasonable. In this sense, transnational call center work serves as a "political project of belonging"[44] through which boundaries between collectivities are constructed and naturalized. Westerners construct themselves as a community of financers whose jobs are being stolen; Indians see themselves as a community of skilled and legitimate participants in the global economy. Western customers, however, can freely express their position on calls, while Indian workers form their community in private, illicit settings. At the same time, as discussed in the next chapter, for Indian workers, realizing that they are seen as objects of hate goes hand in hand with the need to be just like "Westerners."

4

Surveillance Schooling for Professional Clones

Let's go back to the basics. A customer calls with a complaint or query specific to the product or service of the client company. The customer may get impressed with the speed or manner of response, but what he really wants is a satisfactory answer. That does not come from technology—it comes from *knowing,* not just the product, but the customer need, the market scenario, the real end benefit that the customer is looking for, and a familiarity with the marketplace.... A call center handling a tourism product must be manned by people familiar with the tourism industry, and in the same way, one handling process control instrumentation systems must be manned almost exclusively by qualified electronics engineers.[1]

The image of the Indian customer service worker is produced not only by workers themselves but also through a massive coalition of media, government, and business-allied interests within India. The construction of Indian workers as permanently deficient in English (Chapter 2) and as faraway strangers and job thieves (Chapter 3) is juxtaposed with prolific well-crafted statements on Indians as knowledgeable, entrepreneurial, broad-minded, and trainable. This chapter explores the ways in which an economy of familiarity runs through constructions of Indian customer service workers. Like the economy of difference, this is when familiarity is put to work by "involving circuits of production, exchange and consumption."[2] In the case of the Indian customer service industry, familiarity works to create an "imagined kinhood"[3] between workers in India and those in the West. Such a kinhood is enacted through the notion of *professionalism,* which is the term used by media, policy makers, trainers, managers, and workers to refer to the ideal culture that all Indian call centers should strive to inculcate. Professionalism, however, mutates in meaning as it crosses national borders, and while it may refer to work discretion in the West, work processes in India enact professionalism through processes of control. This control is justified in light of what is frequently referred to as India's traditional rather than modern work culture. Discussions of the need for Indian workers to adopt professional cultures in customer service work serve as spaces where normative, hierarchically organized notions of the Western and the traditional are enacted.

Philomena Essed and David Theo Goldberg argue that cultural cloning involves the reproduction of preferences of sameness through productivism, consumerism, and aestheticism.[4] *Productivism* is enacted through the widespread use of seemingly objective performance measures that serve to counter—and in the process construct—nepotism and favoritism as dominant Indian cultural norms. Consumerism and aestheticism occurs when workers self-brand and brand their colleagues as middle-class consumers with a common aestheticism for Western lifestyles. Overall, the image marketing of Indian customer service agents rests on a reification of India as traditional and backward, and the West as progressive and modern. This enactment of the modern and the traditional pervades popular constructions of call center work. Shashi Tharoor, a former UN diplomat and government official notes, for example, that:

> The call centre has become the symbol of India's newly globalised workforce: while traditional India sleeps, a dynamic young cohort of highly skilled, articulate professionals works through the night, functioning on US time under made-up American aliases, pretending familiarity with a culture and climate they've never actually experienced, earning salaries that were undreamt of by their elders (but a fraction of what an American would make) and enjoying a lifestyle that's a cocktail of premature affluence and ersatz westernisation transplanted to an Indian setting.[5]

These attempts at entrenching the dichotomy between traditionalism and westernization is reified, and at times interrupted, by managers, trainers, and call center agents who engage collectively in a continual process of working through similarities and differences between themselves and their employers and customers.

Ideal Jobs for the Model Workforce: Educated, Trainable, and Entrepreneurial

How is the Indian customer service workforce imagined in the eyes of local elites and representatives of Western capital? Following Sara Ahmed, how does Indian culture "become appropriated into the imaginary globality of the colonising nation"?[6] I argue that, through a well-orchestrated public relations machinery, Indians are positioned as a model workforce for transnational service work. Trade—in the context of global capitalist relations that involve the provision of capital from the West and the provision of labor from India—necessitates such an endeavor. This machinery involves the National Association of Software and Service Companies (NASSCOM)—the Indian governmental allied agency set up to promote the subcontracting of information technology and information technology enabled service (IT/ITES) work in India, Western and Indian business media, local business elite who are managers and owner-entrepreneurs at Indian call centers, and workers themselves. Indians are actively produced as ideal service workers who are educated, trainable, and progressive despite their location in a physical and cultural setting that is named as backward, polluted, and tradition-bound. This definition of the "progressive West" through constructions of "traditional India" occurs not only through language training but also via discussions of work processes and organizational cultures. Customer service agents and their managers frequently differentiate their modern, western work environments from traditional Indian ones, while at the same time citing inaccuracies in Western stereotypes about India. In doing so, they give life to the two Indias to which Tharoor refers—a sleeping, traditional India and a progressive, Western, modern one.

In promoting India as an appropriate destination for subcontracted work, managers identify stereotypes about India in the West. One manager claims, "I know a lot of people who don't even know what India is. They still think India is a place where bullock carts are around and snakes are around." Another manager evokes the jungle metaphor: "Say you're a prospective client, you walk into [this company], you have a lot of apprehension... about India. You walk into India, you see elephants, you see cobras walking on the road, you have tigers... You're outsourcing the important part of your business, your customer service. So we take care of the apprehension in terms of technology, in terms of infrastructure, in terms of people, in terms of training." These references to wildlife are intriguing. In an age of global media and travel, most are likely to recognize the absurdity of these constructions of urban India. However, the images evoke the parallel between early Western colonialists facing the dangers of Indian cobras, and contemporary agents in charge of facilitating global economic alliances facing the dangers of poor customer service. Managers easily argue that both fears are unfounded; just as tigers do not roam the streets, Indian workers are skilled service providers. One call center manager stresses the advantages of the Indian workforce by noting that "the common denominator is basic graduation [bachelor's degree] who can speak good, correct English, and who have an energy and enthusiasm, and have...learning capacities." Another manager similarly recounts a positive client response: "We introduce associates [call center workers] to [foreign clients], and they talk to them. They say, '[the associate] speaks with the same accent!'...They're very, very impressed. Extremely impressed."

In these accounts, clients are impressed because their stereotypes of Indians are disrupted. Indians are not strange and backward. In fact, they embody entrepreneurism, energy, and self-determination. As one manager notes,

> The learning curve is very high. People take the job so seriously. We had a girl with a huge Maratha influence [regional accent]. When she joined us, I went back to her and I told [the trainer], this girl is untrainable. But, you know, this girl went back home and she transformed herself to the U.S. [accent], talked to her boyfriend in the U.S. [accent], went to the bathroom and read aloud from papers with the accent, she watched only CNN, she recorded CNN and started pronouncing the words the way the newsreaders pronounced the words. In two months, there was a sea change in her.

This story resonates strongly with colonial attempts to civilize locals through the exposure to Western language and culture. Indians are depicted as hard workers[7] who can quickly compensate for skill deficits. This is an example of the way in which the modern is created through the invention of the traditional. Based on his fieldwork in India, Shehzad Nadeem notes that, "the Indianness of employees is constructed as 'traditional' by employers and managers, as something that is jarringly out of place in today's whirling world. And once this representation of the dilatory and deferent Indian—which borrows heavily from Orientalist discourses—is solidified, the ground is cleared for the creation of the mythic Western professional on native soil."[8] Workers also participate in this invention of the image of the backward, traditional Indian against which their entrepreneurism can be visible. One woman recounts, "I started reading newspapers, then watching English movies. So... it helped me to develop... myself, like, in terms of communication is concerned, how to speak. So... that was a better effort I made. So, I... thought 'yes, I can do that. It's not like it's not possible for me at all,' if you work hard in... where you're lacking." A man describes the challenges he faced when he first joined the call center:

> I was like a bull in a child's shop. I went there and the first week was like hell for me. I couldn't understand what is going on... it was challenging because... unfortunately, they [team members] made it a point that everyday they in some way or the other discourage me that... "what are you doing here, because of you our team is like behind" and all those things. But then that friend of mine, he knew me that once I get into things, I do them. So he taught me, and we had overtimes. So I decide that this is to be done, then that has to be done. There's no excuse for that.

The link between success and entrepreneurism occurs through the valorization of individual achievement. It involves defining one's past self as traditional and therefore lacking, and the educational journey as inherently progressive. This celebration of progressive mindsets is exemplified through reference to the alleged gender equity within India's transnational customer service organizations. Workers as well as managers emphatically deny any relationship between gender and skill. The following manager, for example, explores and then rejects the relationship between gender and work abilities:

> I would presume that collections would be something that guys would be better at, whereas customer service would be something that women would be better, more in terms of being able to be on your feet and empathetic vis-à-vis being assertive and aggressive and being able to make a [collection]. But then again that wouldn't really be true because we have a fair mix of both... Logically, I'd say that collections would be something [pause]

> but then, we have so many women who are really good at that as well. I think it's more in terms of personality, it doesn't really matter about men or women.

In this way, call center workers are depicted as progressive, highly skilled, and trainable—a new breed of Indians pursuing white-collar jobs in the global economy. Like the IT professionals described by Smitha Radhakrishnan as "appropriately Indian," call center workers are significant participants in the process of "cultural streamlining," where the complex strands of Indian culture are transformed into an apolitical, merit-based ideal that is palatable to the West.[9] Despite reports of the repetitive, stressful, and dehumanizing nature of transnational customer service work, these jobs are promoted as highly desirable in India. This privileged position of transnational call centers in the Indian labor market is achieved through pay structures as well as recruitment strategies. Although extremely low in comparison to salaries for similar positions in the West, customer service agents receive considerably higher salaries than those paid in local service industries.[10] In addition to salaries, Indian employees also receive perks such as free transportation, dinners, and gifts for good performance as well as access to onsite cafeterias and recreational facilities.

Recruitment strategies include leafleting at street corners and glossy advertisements placed in national newspapers and college campuses. One such poster covering the walls of a university campus in Pune shows a young man in a suit and tie looking up at the sky. In the accompanying text, students are informed that a placement officer from a large Business Process Outsourcing (BPO) company is visiting the campus—"If you wish to become part of the 19,500 employee strong organization, meet the Wipro BPO Campus Relationship Manager at your campus." Other advertisements lead candidates to training and placement organizations, which form a newly emerging and highly volatile unregulated sector.[11] Jobs are usually depicted as extremely accessible with the promise of "spot offers," openness to "freshers" (undergraduate students), high salaries, and flexible hours. A notice from a training institute distributed on campus contains the headline, "Get your appointment letter before your degree." Another flyer contains an "interview coupon" for a walk-in interview for an international call center job. The slogan "Anyone can apply" is prominently displayed.

There is an immense gulf between the construction of customer service jobs as highly accessible and workers' experiences during the recruitment process. In general, workers describe being selected from hundreds of applicants and interviewed for several rounds, each hours long, before being offered a job. Group interviews remind applicants of the sheer numbers of job hunters. During the selection, success and failure occur in a public forum with consecutive rounds in which unsuccessful candidates are asked to leave. One worker describes the lengthy nature of the process: "I was interviewed for six rounds with [the career consultant], then with [the call center] I interviewed for three rounds. Then I cleared the final interview, then I got the call." Another respondent mentions the strong competition involved in the whole process by reporting that "around 200 people were shortlisted. And out of that 17 people were selected." Workers reported exhaustion and frustration: "You're sitting... with your empty stomach, because in the afternoon, you don't know... if your name comes up and you're gone... So, whole day you are sitting... like a donkey." One worker provides the schedule for the interview:

> [The interview took] seven or eight hours... [They gave me some tests first.] [O]ne was the TOEFL [Test of English as a Foreign Language] test, and then they gave me a small objective type technical test, after that I was also given a one-to-one round, and then she gave me something to read out, maybe to see my accent, to see how I speak. Then I have a detailed questionnaire... I had again a one-to-one round with the technical people. Once I cleared that one, then I had a HR interview. After that HR interview in our company, we get to be interviewed by a vice-president or the CEO of the company... Maybe a hundred people apply and only seven or eight or maximum ten are accepted.

Connections between organizations, career placement firms, and trainers expose potential recruits to deception and harassment. One young woman who was a student pursuing a degree in Engineering responded to an advertisement for a part-time job. After a week of interviews and hours spent waiting for meetings, she was told that only full-time work was available and that she would have to sign a bond stating that she would not leave the job for two years or would be required to repay six months' wages. Reluctant to sign a bond, she approached an employment placement service (referred to as a *consultancy*) seeking part-time work at a call center. After being interviewed for jobs at five different companies, she was told that she was selected to provide service for customers in the U.K. at a large call center. She was required to undergo one week of "training" at the consultancy. On completion of the training she was surprised to learn that she was to again appear for an interview at the call center. After a days' wait at the call center reception area, she was told that the U.K. process had been canceled and that she was now to be trained for a Canadian process. The training would be at the consultancy and would take six months, and she would be paid INR 10,000 (US$217) per month during this time. However, she was fortunate to encounter a past student who informed her that she would be paid only if, at the end of the six-month period, she was successful at an interview at the designated call center. If unsuccessful at the interview she would receive no payment. In addition, she reported that trainers often asked her to go out with them for lunch or dinner, and they advised her to conceal her engineering background to improve her chances of receiving a job offer. They also offered to produce a bogus BSc degree certificate for a fee.

This worker was just one of several who bore the brunt of the collusion of employers, placement services, and trainers in an environment unfettered by enforced regulation. Much more research on systemic barriers enacted through these organizational structures is needed. At present, many call centers do not have the ability or resources to recruit directly and dozens of placement agencies have emerged. These companies are incented by organizations to identify employees who fit certain criteria and are paid a piece rate for each successful candidate. Consultancies also often provide training, for which they might charge prospective workers directly. The terminology used by consultancies serves to confuse and mystify the situation for prospective workers. Consultancies advertise alongside employers, and these two entities are sometimes indistinguishable. In the newspaper classifieds, for example, most advertisements are placed by intermediary organizations promising high-paying careers and 100 percent placements. Individuals are sometimes required to pay a fee to "register," then may be "selected" for training in particular processes. Workers report being told by a consultancy to collect their "offer letter" and instead find that they are in fact attending an interview. Many prospective employees recognize the bind: Consultancies often demand fees for training and provide no guarantee of placement, yet they command a special relationship with employers and may increase their chances of receiving a job offer.

Overall, the recruitment process is experienced by many workers as dehumanizing and humiliating. One respondent describes an unsuccessful interview: "I'm not selected, that they are gonna tell you in front of everybody. So, it's a bit embarrassing." These selective recruitment practices serve not only to name and weed out undesirable workers but also to highlight the aggressive individualism deemed necessary for success in customer service jobs. Successful candidates are those who can display self-promotion, confidence, stamina, and careerism. A recruitment flyer placed in a local newspaper is titled "Get "HIGH" on your job" and reads: "MPhasiS values go beyond professionalism. It is about a company that understands its employee's aspirations and gives them the freedom to follow their dreams." Another box advertisement on the Appointments page poses several questions under the title "Executives Wanted!" Questions include: "Do you enjoy a difficult challenge? Looking for a challenging position offering excellent compensation? Looking to join a fun, fast paced call center with offices in America?" Prospective candidates are invited to "seize the opportunity." These ideal characteristics are also stated in companies' "quality policies" as evident in the following example of a written company policy:

> We will encourage meritocracy based on talent and performance
> Rewards and Recognition will be differentiated and will be a consequence of an individual's performance
> We will encourage leadership at every level by promoting entrepreneurial thinking.[12]

There remains, however, an uncanny paradox between the ideal traits of workers as described above and the actual format of interviews. Respondents almost uniformly note that they have no control over the interview process. Many report being made to wait for up to ten hours with no advance warning. When asked about the likely reasons for their success or failure, respondents make vague guesses and say they were given no formal feedback. Indeed, many workers such as the one quoted above talk about feeling "like a donkey"—drawing attention to their awareness of their sanctioned powerlessness during the interview process. For call center workers, the aggressive individualism required as part of their jobs coexists with the need for a passive acceptance of authority and tolerance for uncertainty.

Some workers attributed their success in obtaining their jobs to their accents or grammar, as noted in Chapter 2. Others identified their fit with call center work cultures. Among those excluded from the BPO industry, one woman who was unsuccessful in obtaining a job in the sector despite a convent education explains the industry preference for "dudes and babes":

> They find dudes and babes better than people like me, normal people like me. That's what I've seen, you know, many places where I've been, these people, the dudes who are like actually wearing rings in their ears, or had those funky... They were picked up. Then, the girls who were wearing like really less clothes... these people used to be called in first. Like, we were standing in a line. It was long queue... it was a very hot day. We were standing outside and these people were like, "come, girls, this, this, this, this, you come in, you come in." Just by looking at them, and I was like, what is happening? So, should I wear less clothes and come from tomorrow for giving interview [laugh]? That was one thing which came in mind. Because they need people who are dudes, because the people who look like that can speak better English. I think that's what their point of view is... they prefer girls who are like babes, who can... maybe they think these people adjust more... better.

Overall, respondents experience access to call center jobs as elusive and largely based on chance. Many also describe the interview process as humiliating and stressful in light of job advertisements that highlight accessibility. These practices serve to further brand jobs as highly desirable and requiring workers who are progressive and entrepreneurial. This construction of the ideal worker occurs not only at the point of entry but also through the labor process in place at call centers, specifically via the notion of "professionalism."

Enacting Professionalism

Aside from the images of happy Western look-alikes on advertisements, call center jobs are also constructed as desirable through the liberal use of the notion of "professionalism" in training materials and organizational discourses. Western ideologies of professionalism conjure up images of worker discretion, independent decision-making, expertise, and temporal autonomy.[13] Premilla D'Cruz and Ernesto Noronha note that in Indian call centers, however, the notion of professionalism serves primarily as a form of disciplinary control.[14] Ideals of professionalism are at the heart of the work that workers do to fashion themselves into ideal transnational customer service providers. Workers perform "identity work" by presenting themselves in particular ways, and constructing their "identity at work" by negotiating their day-to-day interactions to attempt to control how they are perceived.[15] One worker describes her attempt to define the professionalism required in her job:

> It's that serious, believe me. Where I work, I have to be in a trouser and in a shirt every single day... you always have to be prim and proper. You have to be your best, you have to look your best when you go to work... I told my boyfriend, "in fact, you'll be surprised the girl who owns [B—mall], she works with me. You'll be surprised about the kind of girls that work with me. Some of them are so decent, I can't tell you."... [C]ome see the code of conduct. Come see the kind of people there are. Come see the kind of discipline—you won't find it in any other organization.

The "code of conduct" refers to a strict time discipline (as discussed in Chapter 6) as well as a requirement to be polite and patient in the face of abusive callers (as discussed in Chapter 5). However, the most central aspect of this "code of conduct" is the notion of professionalism in call centers that serves to highlight similarities between the norms of Indian call center agents in India and their customers or employers in the West. Parallels between Western work norms and cultures in Indian call centers are created through *aestheticism* (depiction of the workspace as a pristine space of equal opportunities), *productivism* (organization of work in terms of scripts, teams, and performance appraisals), and *consumerism* (construction of work as fun). These are key elements of cloning culture, which serves to enact a particular kind of kinhood, or similarity between India and the West. Goldberg and Essed note that aestheticism contributes to cloning culture through the reproduction of taste preferences, productivism through the creation of the image of an ideal worker, and consumerism via the assumptions of shared identities through leisure preferences.[16] In each of these expressions of the "professionalism" within transnational call centers, distinctions between the modern and the traditional are enacted.

Aestheticism: The Pocket of Western Space

Customer service agents occupy a unique physical and temporal space within India. Workers describe their organizations as pockets of Western space because a strong demarcation is maintained between the work-life in India and the work-life within a call center. In terms of the organization of the workspace, one worker notes, "I think the way they have set up the workspace is pretty much similar to what they have in North America. Because I have seen offices in North America, there's not much of a difference. You have a monitor, you have the whole setup in front of you, you have your own desk in there, you have your own notice board, you wanna put up something, you can do it. It's pretty comfortable and you do enjoy that." In a similar way, Winifred Poster describes the physical layout of a customer service organization in India: "The office space is... decorated with many reminders and guides of American culture, such as maps of U.S. states, and grammar school-type collages (which workers have made themselves) presenting facts and information about particular regions."[17] This décor serves to mark not only continuity with the West but also discontinuity with India. Indian workspaces are depicted as unclean, disorganized, bureaucratic, and nepotistic. One worker describes his workplace: "It is not like a 'lala' [casual/orthodox/traditional] type of company, working in the government type of organizations, you know, just to pass a file. You have to do all sort of things. If a work has to be done, it has to be done." The parallel to cultures of government are significant given the historic associations between the civil service and middle-class status. However, the civil service is characterized as backward and antithetical to professionalism in call centers:

> Apart from BPO, I think it will still take another ten years to go to the level of getting out of favoritism and, you know, falling into that pure competitiveness, though government is trying that because government two years ago had stopped the rule of only seniors getting promoted. Even the bribes and everything is being stopped because now you have counters and surveillance and cameras so that has been reduced to a large extent. So, things

are happening around. It will take another ten years in Pune at least. But it surely is developing.

Workplaces are seen as progressive because of their cleanliness, organizational order, and equal opportunity. They stand out against the social landscape, assumed to comprise organizations that are dirty and backward. One worker makes explicit links among order, cleanliness, decency, and health, describing his workplace as "very clean and very decent. It's very spacious, very hygienic, very clean."[18] Normative hierarchies are enacted through the linking of cleanliness with decency in the characterizations of Westernized workspaces. As Essed and Goldberg note, "converging discriminations *against* particular groups are also indicative of normative preferences *for* clones of imagined perfection of the same type and profile."[19] As a CEO of a large Indian IT firm comments, "when you come to our campus [workplace], you are leaving India behind."[20] This construction of space as "Western" is epitomized in the flat organizational structure of the call center which, once again, is contrasted to the hierarchical character of Indian society. Workers note,

> Everyone is treated equally in call centers. See, even I am working in the same post, she is a graduate, I am undergraduate. She is also working on the same post.... [T]he best part of call centers which I like, you know, there is no partiality. See, you belong to a same rule, I belong to a same rule. There's nothing called "Auntie, aap kar sakte ho mere liye." [Auntie, can you do this for me?] No way! I never say: "Boss, can I do this?" "Boss, can I... do this?" No. Call him name. He is elder to you or younger to you. Forget it. All guys are equally treated. The best part is that. The way I am born and brought up... being in a joint family, I have to call everyone uncle, aunt, and all.

> Generally, these call centers are very professional... because they have to meet the U.S. clients' requirements. Generally, if you have a manager in India, who thinks what you are thinking, it will be a little easier to kind of get into favoritism or, like, if my manager is thinking the same I am thinking and I can... kind of butter him... and get my promotions. But the manager himself has a manager who is in U.S. and who doesn't think the way he is thinking. So they have to be very professional. They give equal chances to people who really want to work and who really can work. So they have to, like, really be at their foot to find out who is doing good and who is not. That's why we have

> performance appraisals. It's totally based on how you perform and that's what decides your future. They are really professional. Because if they are not, they have their U.S. managers who are there to kind of screw them up.

Joint families and alliances based on caste, creed, color, or religion are defined as backward practices endemic of a traditional India. They foster nepotism, false respect, and a failure to take responsibility for oneself.[21] In contrast, call center workers are required to go against the "way they were brought up" and become entrepreneurial, independent workers. One worker notes that given the central role of performance indicators and decentralized management, it is difficult for senior staff to distribute rewards on the basis of prejudice: "There are various circumstances you have... like caste, creed, color, religion. But in this company, I've seen that it's not there. They don't have any such politics. Because they have score cards, so they have to go accordingly. It was not only in the hands of the manager himself." In these ways, workers reproduce the rhetoric that constructs India as traditional and the West as progressive. At the same time, as workers discuss the experiences of their work, it becomes clear that there is a significant gap between the actual and professed ideals of Western professionalism.

Cloning Productivism

Descriptions of work processes in call centers in the United Kingdom, United States, Canada, and Australia bear an uncanny resemblance to those in India. In some ways, call center organizational processes seem to have been exported intact. Despite the fact that customer service is a relatively new industry in India, there is a degree of uniformity across various individual centers. Diane van den Broek describes five control strategies used in Australian call centers: (1) open office designs, (2) automated call queuing, (3) large visual displays of individual and team productivity, (4) daily computer-generated reports on each employee's performance, and (5) quality assessments through knowledge performance indicators determined through customer satisfaction reports, barging [listening to calls while they are in progress], and computing average handling times.[22] These strategies seem to be mirrored in workers' descriptions of their places of work, which is not surprising because Western clients dictate work norms.

The rigidity of performance practices typical of call centers worldwide do not sit comfortably with ideals of Western professionalism. Workers continually mediate the requirement to be professional with the pressure to "perform." The twin mantras of professionalism and performance have to be continually reconciled in the requirements for scripting, teamwork, and performance measures. These work processes form an arena within which workers are required to perform authenticity work through which they are professional and able to provide service to Western customers.

Enactments and Reversals in Scripted Taylorism Interviews conducted in the early and mid-2000s revealed a widespread prevalence of scripted Taylorism, or the repetitive use of predefined phrases during each call.[23] Workers report either being given exact scripts to follow or being asked to read from computer screens, or even, in the most liberal cases, being asked to use their own words to convey specific information. One worker describes an interesting example of how scripted Taylorism works: "This is our script, we have to go through this: 'Thank you for choosing [name of American company]. My name is Tanya [assigned pseudonym]. May I have your first and last name? Thank you. May I call you by your first name? Thank you very much. How are you doing today?'... These are the typical statements that we have to say: 'Great. Thank you. Excellent. Wonderful job.' These are the power words. We have to use those words in our scripts."

Scripts eliminate the need for any decision making while reducing the variety of customer responses. Justifications for scripting are peppered with stereotypes of traditional, unimaginative, backward Indians. Laurie Cohen and Amal El-Sawad's research on constructions of Indian customer service representatives by U.K.–based colleagues working for the same company reveals that Indians are frequently depicted as children who require monitoring. One U.K.–based respondent they interviewed notes that, "if you take your eye off the ball then things slip up a wee bit and they go back to whatever the old way was of doing things." Other U.K.–based team members reveal that the team directs the easiest work to India. Indians are constructed as "bright and friendly, yet somewhat muddled and childlike subordinate, in need of close monitoring and on-going control."[24] Scripts provide opportunities for such control.

In other settings, service scripts have been found to help workers enforce their will over their customers and distance themselves from disagreeable interactions.[25] Indian call center workers, however, uniformly experience scripts as de-skilling, repetitive, and tedious. A worker interviewed in 2002 notes that, "It's not that you are using your own words. You have to use these standard scripts. You have to use these same sentences.... You're like a keyed toy.... We were just told that we had to do the standard scripts. Just stick to your standard scripts." While scripting in customer service work facilitates control of information, it is also acknowledged to interfere with opportunities to build rapport between workers and customers. As Monica Heller summarizes, "service providers are meant to reach clients 'in their own language'... but since clients rarely only come in one size, it is difficult to find standardized routines that correspond to a wide variety of ways of speaking... [T]he new work order produces paradoxes or contradictions between standardization and authenticity."[26] The need to negotiate this contradiction between authenticity and standardization is widely cited by the Indian customer service workers interviewed after 2005. Rather than an emphasis on scripted Taylorism, these later interviews report formal and informal organizational norms that downplay scripts.[27] A worker interviewed in 2007, for example, describes a typical call where he says, "I've just given the opening, 'Hello Mrs. Smith, my name is Raymond Douglas. I am calling you from [company name]. So, how can I help you today?' My part is finished. Script is finished. Then, she'll ask me questions." Another worker recounts a conversation with his manager on the inefficiency of scripts: "I cannot be a robot. You make me sit and you'll tell me do that, do that, do this.' I also have my own explanation. I have my own experience, let me apply it. As long as you're getting benefit, it's all right. You're not... having any problem, you're not getting a D-Sat [score given by a dissatisfied customer], leave it on me, why are you worried of it?" Another agent describes the instructions he was given on scripting during training. His team was asked to listen to calls made by a model employee who did not follow the script required by the official policy of the company. Rather than being reprimanded, this behavior was valorized: "[He] used to avoid the script, means that is illegal, means that was the wrong thing he was doing. And even the Unit Manager knew that, means he was doing wrong, but... it is called smart work. It is called smart work. So you should be able to do smart work."

This trend away from scripting suggests that customer service work has become more complex, requiring a broader range of skills.[28] One manager provides a historical analysis on the use of scripts by noting, "As a customer, I'll never be impressed [by scripts]. . . . I definitely can understand that the person is reading from somewhere . . . now each and every call center is adapting to this, doing away with verbiage, scripts. If you hire a person, you have confidence in him, maybe you hire those who are highly educated, definitely you know that this person can easily construct a sentence, you just need to give him the points which he needs to cover."

Whether implicitly sanctioned or officially required, many of the workers interviewed after 2005 highlight the expectation that they are required to exercise script discretion on calls by focusing on the need to "build rapport" with customers. Scripting is acknowledged to lead to customer dissatisfaction and backlash:[29] "If I call up someone in a customer service and if that particular agent is sounding scripted, I won't be satisfied. I should hear that call as a natural call. So the client wants me to be natural and not scripted."

In the context of the extensive use of performance measures, such a movement away from scripts, however, leads to considerable uncertainty about work expectations. Workers answering up to several hundred calls a day note the stress of having to say exactly what is required while simultaneously conveying information with constant variations in a way that seems natural: "At training time, we were given a script. When we hit the floor, when we started taking calls for a few days, we just follow the script. But later on . . . you should not be verbatim. If you're verbatim, no one will listen to you. So, you have to be different, you have to be innovative." While this demand to "be innovative" might suggest a degree of worker control typical of professional work in the West, agents in India are commanded to be unscripted in much the same way as they were earlier commanded to be scripted. The relaxation in use of scripts is accompanied by increased monitoring.[30] Indeed, as the use of scripts seems to have waned in many Indian call centers in recent years, the monitoring mechanisms seem to have intensified in terms of their complexity and precision. The need for workers who adhere to Western notions of professionalism *but do not seem scripted to do so* justifies the control over every aspect of the work process in Indian call centers.

Scoring Performance Through monitoring, workers' performance is scored on a continual basis. These scores are translated directly into financial benefits that workers receive as part of their monthly salaries.

The actual conversion of performance into scores, however, involves a task of mind-boggling complexity. Workers not only have to understand the multiple dimensions along which they are evaluated (e.g., call handling time, customer satisfaction, accent, communication skills) but also need to balance various measures to calculate the most beneficial outcomes in their work. In addition, workers have no mechanism to challenge assigned performance scores. By and large, the professed transparency of work processes and performance appraisals in call centers remains largely rhetorical, and workers instead discuss the confusion and uncertainty they feel regarding the way in which their work is evaluated.

As is characteristic of call centers around the world, daily data is automatically generated on the average handling time of each agent. Customers are also surveyed for C-SAT (customer satisfaction) scores to be calculated. As yet another component of the evaluation, quality inspectors "barge into," or listen undetected, to calls of each agent. Then each call is scored on various quality dimensions such as accent, information provided, and deference. One worker describes the cumulative effect of these measures:

> That is the pressure in the job. It is a psychologically . . . I mean, even though we are not doing anything physically, physical exercise . . . It's tremendous psychological pressure that we go through. First of all, understanding that person over the phone and giving the quality expectations. The quality that we have . . . like, we have three different quality measures. First is the technical resolution that you're giving. Ultimately, is the customer able to get the Internet or not? . . . And if you had given the correct resolution, was there any other way to give it more quicker? Second is the voice and accent part of it, how did you speak to the customer . . . did you lose your temper . . . how good you were in a human level with the customer. Then, for that, another manager is sitting there as a voice and accent manager. The third is the AHT [average handling time] part of it, how quicker you are giving the resolution.

As the quote above reveals, monitoring is based on highly subjective measures such as connecting with customers. Yet, performance incentives are based on seemingly objective scores. Scores are a "non-living actor" in call center organizations.[31] Scores do not simply measure performance; rather, team leaders and workers modify their behaviors so that they work in ways that are visible in the scores. The ease with which most customer service workers were able to recount the details of the tools used to assess the quality of their work suggests their active engagement with these measures. One respondent shared a written document entitled "The Performance Matrix," which was used by evaluators to score performance. The Performance Matrix contains six lettered sections:

A. Call opening
B. Program compliance
C. Communication
D. Product knowledge
E. Selling skills
F. Accuracy

Within each section, there are two to eleven items, each with a score of 1 point. These items include criteria such as "does not change order of script," "makes second attempt to capture information," "refrains from using any extra verbiage," "listens to the customer appropriately," "does not interrupt and overtalk," "should not have any regional influence," "should enunciate words correctly," "does not use filler words such as 'well,' 'alright,' 'OK,'" "displays confidence," "has intonation, inflection, and enthusiasm," "transitions quickly and effectively through the call," and "handles DNC [Do Not Call] request appropriately."

Based on the sheer number of criteria for evaluation, scoring becomes a highly subjective task. In addition, the time required to evaluate a call on such a large number of minute details is likely to be many times more than the call itself. This monitoring device, therefore, promotes a panoptic approach to evaluation where scores are based on the review of a handful of calls from the several thousand an agent may receive on a monthly basis. As a result, despite the rhetoric of fairness and transparency, many respondents experience performance evaluation as a matter of luck. As one worker reports, "There is a quality team, which monitors your call. So, for a new person, I think...fifteen of your calls are monitored every month, and for a tenured operator, I think four to five calls are monitored. Randomly. So if you are lucky, you're lucky. If you are not, you're not. It's like that. You see, four calls you score a 100, fifth call you score a 0. So divide 400 by 5. So, instead of getting a 100, you get 80. It is below 85. So 2,000 rupees gone." In spite of this element of luck, consequences of poor scores are severe: "There is no job security in our case. It all depends on our performance. If you perform well, you can stick to the company. If you are not performing at any time, they can throw you out of the company."

The actual conversion of scores into incentives is also problematic. None of the workers interviewed were unionized but several observed unfair employment practices through the masking of the calculation in their incentive structures. One worker characterizes the organizational climate as follows: "When you go on the floor, when you start taking calls, your salary is much more than what you are supposed to get in training because you have a lot of incentives. They don't explain why they are deducting so much money. They'll make up some or the other excuse.... If you create a lot of uproar [about this]... you get blacklisted." Others report that despite the individual evaluations, incentives are, in fact, comparatively assigned. As a result, high scores do not always translate into high incentives. One respondent, for example, said that her colleague received a INR 2,000 incentive for a score of 90.3, while she received a INR 1,000 incentive for a score of 90.2. Another respondent explains that companies monitor a higher number of calls when agents receive high scores so that they can find calls that will reduce their overall score: "If your one call is 100% they barge your second call, third call. So they try to maintain one or two people get high incentives."

Overall, respondents seemed keenly aware that, while it was in the company's interest to have all agents performing well, there was considerable pressure not to increase labor costs. As a result, agents noted that performance requirements increase as agents gain skill and experience.

Competing Teams Incentive structures are closely tied to the particular form of team-based work prevalent in call centers. Diane van den Broek, George Callaghan, and Paul Thompson term this approach "teams without teamwork."[32] Team structures serve largely to engender competition as well as to monitor and control workers. In BPOs, teamwork is widely constructed as a sign of professionalism, as the following worker explains: "They used to talk about your work, about how you have to grow, what you can do, what you cannot do. It was all professional environment, you can say. We were a team working of thirty people. We were a group of thirty people working together as a team. It makes you work together as a team."

Teams "work together" by competing with other teams for scores that translate into perks such as shopping vouchers. When asked to describe the meaning of professionalism in teamwork, the respondent quoted above goes on to refer to the monitoring function of the team: "They need to know am I disposing the calls properly, am I talking to the customers properly. We used to have quality feedback every week. They used to listen to our calls. They used to tell you, 'on this call, you do not do this, you should do this.' We always had a Team Leader who used to give us feedback. It was never like you are boss or something. You're always a leader, a person who could teach you, a person who you could learn from. We're always open to learning." The focus on teamwork thus emphasizes the construction of call centers as spaces of equal opportunity. This approach mimics the work organization at call centers in the West and serves to standardize customer service because Indian workers can be made just like those in the West. Mimicry, however, is always accompanied by slippage.[33] Professional workers in India are expected to be entrepreneurial and "always open to learning" yet defer to the authority of their team leaders and managers.

Dancing Around Scores Managerial strategies of control do not go unchallenged by individual workers. Nadeem notes that the Indian call center worker who is a "deferent worker, fresh out of school, buffeted by managerial demands for professionalism, enacts a unique form of individualism—that partakes of contrasting qualities—workers can be surprisingly servile and astonishingly assertive."[34] This combination of servitude and assertiveness occurs among service workers in a variety of contexts.[35] Indian customer service workers develop work strategies to maximize their performance scores in the context of the routinized processes that they have to follow. To achieve the highest performance scores, workers need to resolve customer issues quickly. By doing so, they can meet their quotas, receive positive feedback from customers, and ensure that customers do not call back within a certain period of time. Workers recognize that maximizing performance scores can sometimes be achieved without fully meeting customers' needs. As one worker notes, "people they'll just talk very good. They talk about the weather. They give wrong information to the customer, but they get very good C-Sat." At times workers develop strategies that reduce their stress without negatively impacting their scores, such as the use of unnecessary holds to ensure a manageable pace on the job; one worker reports that "while talking [to customers], we make comments [to each other], so we don't feel sleepy [laughs]. We put passengers on a hold, and we naturally chat with each other [both laugh]. And we [say] 'you just give us a few moments, so that we can just check out the information for you,' and we just put the [customer] on hold... [In] that time, like, we can make fun over here."

Workers also perform complex calculations and sometimes sacrifice their scores on one of the performance dimensions to increase their scores on others. For example, agents encourage customers to wait for forty-eight hours for a resolution since some companies provide incentives only if customers do not call back within this period. As one respondent summarizes, "The more you bluff, the more you gain." To speed up calls, workers often assess the length of time an issue is likely to take for resolution. This assessment depends on the problem at hand as well as on the mood of the customer. In cases where issues are complicated and customers are irate, workers sometimes decide to give customers a *talla*, or hoax solution. These strategies involve continually assessing customer responses in light of performance measures. One worker describes his decision-making process, "You have to judge the person... [a]ccording to whether he is very much irritated, whether he wants to resolve the issue.... If you find a person, like, he is very much irritated, and you know, you cannot deal within twenty minutes, so just ask him, 'Sir, will it do if I call you after 48 hours? Because I will try to research the issue properly.' And if he says, 'Yes, fine, 48 hours.' You don't call him back after 48 hours.' Another agent similarly notes: "When you get a call you have to decide in the first fifteen, twenty minutes... how long is this call likely to take.... If you know it's going to be a very difficult call, it's kind of like better for you to hang it up... finish it quickly."

Such employee practices are surprising given that calls are continuously and randomly monitored by supervisors for consistency and quality purposes. Technology is not only a tool of managerial control but also can be manipulated for workers' benefit, especially when workers have four-year undergraduate degrees in programming or engineering as some customer service agents do.[36] One call center worker mentions that he knows when his supervisor is listening to his calls: "As soon as they 'barge into' the call, you hear a beep sound like THIS [very soft and low beep]. So we get to know that now the call is being recorded. OK, so there's a certain time, like, he's going to record the call for five minutes or ten minutes." In general, highly routinized performance measurement tools provoke workers to maximize their scores without actually providing solutions to customers even when workers may be fully competent and knowledgeable on the issues that customers need resolved.

Workers also use technology to familiarize themselves with wages and working conditions in the West. Despite competitive and individualist performance appraisal mechanisms, workers often form informal alliances to exchange information.[37] Despite their knowledge that they are doing the "same" work as done by workers in the West, there is a keen awareness of their differential pay. While call center workers are paid high salaries in comparison to the remuneration provided in other service-sector jobs in India, they still note that call center salaries are far lower than the wages often paid in professional jobs in the Indian labor market. A worker justifies his characterization of call center work as poorly paid by saying, "I have a buddy of mine, he is having four years of experience as a software developer and because of this slack he [had to leave]. He was earning around INR 25,000 [US$545). And, at this point in time [at the call center], he might be earning maximum INR 8,000 [US$175]."

Considering that workers were repeatedly told that they were fortunate to have clean, white-collar, professional jobs with multinational corporations, and that they are paid high salaries, the women and men interviewed for this book highlighted the benefits that both American companies and Indian subcontractors extract from their labor. The detailed knowledge that workers possess of the differential salaries are evidence that we are living in a "world of flows" characterized by "objects in motion";[38] these objects include ideas, people, goods, images, and technologies. While call center workers in India are trained to take on Western personas, learn about the West, and live on Western time, they also gain a broader awareness of their positions in the global labor market because of their connection to Western labor markets and the global economic relations within which their jobs are situated. As one worker notes, "If you think about [call center] jobs there [in the United States], they would be paying at least ten or fifteen dollars per hour for a fresh person. So per hour means if you work eight hours, you calculate it would be around, like, a hundred and fifty dollars per day they have to pay. That's... like legislated minimum wage, not for people with any experience."

In these ways, customer service workers draw attention to cultures of cloning by making reference to the similarities between customer service work done in the West and in India. They also note that Indian workers are paid less for the same work. Interestingly, the familiarity is put to work, although to different ends by managers and workers. From the supervisory perspective, managers stress that Indians can become as professional as Westerners through the correct monitoring and training. The primary benefit of outsourcing—lower labor costs—can then be achieved. In contrast, workers note that they are just like Western workers but do not receive the same benefits. These claims of familiarity, however, are enacted as well as challenged through the discourses of consumerism running through discussions of call center work. In these discussions, work is constructed to be consumed just like other activities associated with fun.

Consuming Work as Fun

There are two ways in which consumerism structures customer service workers' experiences. First, workers often self-brand and brand one another as India's new middle class recognizable by their patterns of consumption. Second, their work is itself packaged as "fun" in order to be consumed alongside parties and games. These strategies facilitate the continual inscription of Western professionalism as modern and progressive. Workers do not unanimously endorse this link between work and fun, and many draw attention to the construction of work as fun as having discursive power to highlight as well as mask aspects of their jobs. They do this, however, by reifying the assumed connection between the West and the culture of fun and argue instead for recognition of Indian traditions and cultures. In this way, the professionalism enacted through construction of work as fun serves as another arena where the dichotomy between the progressive West and backward India is brought to life.

Call center workers are part of India's new middle class, which is a social group defined primarily by its practices of consumption that mirror Western consumer culture.[39] New middle-class lifestyles are characterized by the focus on leisure and service activities such as restaurants and nightclubs. As Mathangi Krishnamurthy summarizes, "the call center is... the site where a simultaneous construction of the two interlocking figures of producer and consumer is taking place."[40] This link between production and consumption is more pronounced than in most other occupations in India given that a majority of call center workers are young, and many are reputed to spend a high percentage of their incomes on entertainment and leisure. One worker highlights the consumption power of many call center workers by saying that they "can spend a very lavish life, luxurious and chill out in every pub in the weekends and have couple of drinks, can go on for dates."

As discussed in the beginning of this chapter, call center workers are marketed by the Indian media and business elite as an ideal transnational workforce because they "wear this brand" of the consumer worker on a daily basis. Wearing a brand takes work because employees have to maintain "daily practice at expressing the brand's conceptual attributes,"[41] and this affects how they experience their jobs as well as conceptualize themselves. One worker describes his social life: "[I] go out for parties, chill out, go for movies. It is good earning and spending. Earnings of five days and spending on the weekends. It is U.S. culture, I would say." Ideal workers are expected to have "an amiable personality, a childish playfulness, a happy-go-lucky frame of mind and an extroverted and carefree demeanor."[42] This juxtaposition of earning and spending is seen both as characteristic of U.S. culture and as related to professionalism. As one agent notes, "It is cool; we don't feel like getting out of there because one of the things is that you are working with the very young crowd and you are part of it, who has just passed out of the college, and the people who have same thoughts, you are working with them.... Very professional environment, very, at the same time, it is very fun. The whole environment is very cool."

Not all workers experience their work environments in this way. Several respondents note that the culture of fun and social connection also facilitates favoritism. One woman summarizes that only through "flattering someone [can] you become something." Several male workers refer to the differential treatment of women; one man observes, for example, that "girls have been given more opportunities. And the guys who are very close to the team leaders, they have been given opportunities." Other workers explicitly refer to personal, often sexualized relations between team leaders and workers: "Like TLs [team leaders] usually taking care of girls in their team...'it's ok, you take your break, you can extend your break.' But if a guy...if my break is for just twenty minutes, I extended for twenty-five minutes, he'll start shouting at you, yelling at you, 'why you are late?' And if a girl extends, 'it's ok, sit down, sit down.' Then this guy will go on off days with her for coffee or for a movie."

Peter Fleming notes the prevalence of "fun projects" as a form of informal managerial control in call centers in Australia. He argues that managed fun initiatives such as parties, playfulness, and games are an "easier way to adjust the worker to exploitative and otherwise alienating work processes [because] fun seldom disrupts the ground-zero principle of capital accumulation." Some workers in Australian call centers recognize the "patronizing and mawkishly paternalistic flavor" of this management approach and see the fun rhetoric as shallow and fake.[43] Workers in Indian call centers who are critical of the fun discourses often link these discourses to Western culture—cultures of fun are seen as characteristic of Western professional culture. These workers name their colleagues' acceptance of Western leisure activities and dress codes as a betrayal. One agent comments on the behavior of his colleagues: "They are moving toward the Western culture. They are getting bad, that's what happens in all call centers. It's not good. It's not good. We Indian people have some great regards, we are being respected by our tradition and culture. We have to maintain it. You are just talking to a U.K. customer... you cannot adopt their culture. If you are in India, you have to follow your culture." Comments often characterize Western cultures as emphasizing fun and money: "These guys fall into excessive smoking. They practice all kinds of different stunts [like] grass [marijuana] and *charas* [hashish] and... they feel that by doing these things, they are, you know, becoming... they are mirroring those Westernized guys." These workers romanticize and homogenize Indian traditionalism and contrast it to Western cultures of fun: "The culture over here is such... you talk about dollars, about plastic money. Everything, the terms, the terminology, is more like the U.S. over here. Even if you're talking to somebody over there, in U.S., you don't feel that you are in India. The way they dress, the girls nowadays, everybody's in trousers, short skirts, formal shoes. The way they walk. Everything is changed, Westernized, everything. Talking, eating, girls smoking."

Workers construct Indian culture as traditional, family oriented, and nonmaterialist. This explains the seemingly contradictory trends of economic globalization and religious conservatism in recent Indian politics. Evoking central tenets of Hinduism, such as the need to be nonmaterial and unselfish, workers justify the often demeaning conditions of their work.[44] This link between Hinduism and India's economic liberalization is accompanied by the explicit reference of Muslim practices as regressive, rigid, and threatening. Indeed, while some workers object to the smoking and drugs assumed to arise from Western influences in call centers, others note the need to mask their religious convictions. One man, a practicing Muslim, recounts his unsuccessful attempts to avoid working in a process (insurance) that violates his religious practice. He keeps his religious beliefs secret at work: "There is no religion over there [at the workplace]. You are just a worker—a worker of an organization. If I tell this [about my religious beliefs] over there, they will think I am really backward and all. That's how the BPOs work . . . you have to be very professional. You have to be very limited. Whatever they have taught us, same thing you have to do. You don't have to add anything." Being "limited," in this context, involves enacting a form of professionalism that brackets workers' social and cultural contexts. The only sanctioned crossing of the work–life boundary is the emulation of the ideal of the fun-seeking, Westernized, consumerist youth worker.

Even young, single workers who fall closest to this ideal, however, often challenge the common depiction of call centers as "fun" places to work, as an extension of college life with opportunities for leisure, disposable income, and engagement with popular culture. Workers recognize that performance measures themselves are constructed as games with "prizes" and "rewards."[45] Indeed, the aesthetic of fun often serves as an indirect form of worker control where competitions, games, and prizes are intended to increase productivity by engendering individual competition. As one worker notes,

> A lot of people think it's a fun job. A lot of people have this myth that it is fun. Everybody says when you're in training, it's like a honeymoon with every company. But it's not like that because there's stress, there's insecurity. If you don't clear your test, you're going to be sacked. A lot of people have this myth that BPOs, if you don't get through one, you'll get through another. But it is not like that. It's just not like that. Because there's no security. If you're not good, if you're not a consistent performer, you're sacked. Your scores have to be intact. How you interact with people. Because this is the people's industry. You have to be good with your colleagues; at the same time, you have to see your hours of production. So everything—you can't take your breaks for granted. You can't come late. You can't walk in when you want, and if you're a second late, there's trouble. You are issued a

warning letter. Three warnings if you're still not improving, you're sacked. So it's a lot.... You have to give your 100 percent. Ninety percent also doesn't do. So it's not as easy as it seems.

As this quote reveals, workers are not always convinced by constructions of their workplaces as fun; the relationship between productivity and games is complex and often does not result in a simplistic compliance with company directives. Workers are fully aware of the link between fun projects and productivity: "The managers and the TLs [team leaders] are exploiting this kind of thing. They know that tomorrow, they'll have to work for twelve hours. 'O.K., come, could we all have a party? We'll have a jam session'...these are...gestures...indirect bribes." Indirect bribes are sometimes self-funded, and those who fail to participate risk not being seen as team players.[46]

Alongside the focus on "fun" in call centers, there is the parallel between work and school. Workers often describe their organizations as school-like spaces and note that they sometimes spend their breaks playing games (such as table tennis) or eating with friends. At the same time, however, there is a widespread recognition that workers are constructed as students in other, more paternalistic ways. Workers are seen as irresponsible youth who require discipline and remedial training. For example, respondents report having to do monthly written tests that play a role in determining their incentives; these tests involve memorizing correct responses to customer queries. For minor transgressions (such as chatting with one another or taking unscheduled washroom breaks), workers note that they are often "shouted at" by their team leaders.

The relationship between schooling and employment has been explored by social reproduction theorists, who have noted that schools often inculcate the social relations of production in capitalism.[47] Hierarchies between students and teachers serve to make subordination routine. Schooling, however, is not only influenced by capitalism but also iteratively constructs the relations of production within jobs whereby ideologies of schooling and discipline pervade customer service jobs. One worker describes his job by noting, "BPO is not even a job. It's like you're in school. You're monitored. You can't laugh loudly. You can't talk loudly. You have to get up at this time. You have to sleep at this time. You have no life. You have to be in a certain way at a certain time. If you exceed your break by one minute, a warning letter is issued."

Peter McLaren argues that schools function to teach students the importance of disciplining their "unruly" bodies so as to allow for effective learning. This is referred to as the process of "enfleshment" whereby disciplinary practices do not just "sit on the surface of the flesh but are . . . embedded in the flesh" so that they structure how students think about their own bodies.[48] Work norms based on such authoritative exercise of discipline parallel the exercise of discipline on marginalized youth in schools. As institutions, schools serve as sites of socialization where poor youth come to accept responsibility for the conditions of their poverty. They are encouraged to link their lack of economic success to their individual failure, rather than to the social and economic structure of capitalism.[49] In a similar way, customer service representatives are held responsible for their performance targets with no regard for external constraints. Implicit is the construction of performance as an objective, value-free measure. In addition, training primarily serves to reinforce workers' sense of themselves as children who require supervision, monitoring, and reprimand. In the call centers, supervisors are referred to as "monitors" with authority to train workers and oversee their productivity. Like in schools, monitors in call centers often relate to workers through processes of shame and fear. Nadeem documents the experiences of a top-performing employee who was terminated because of "lapses" such as "returning from the bathroom one minute and fifty seconds late."[50] Poster observes that performance scores are posted at the entrance for all employees to compare.[51]

These disciplinary strategies serve to transform Indian call center workers into "professionals" who possess the time discipline central to Western work norms. Cloning through aestheticism, productivism, and consumerism aim to compensate for assumed backwardness of Indian work culture. In this context, Indian consumerist and middle-class identities of privilege exist alongside the construction of workers as childlike and needy of supervision, monitoring, and structure. These processes, however, are filled with gaps and ironies, and workers' accounts reflect their experiences, which are far from the unproblematic cloning of Western identities, work cultures, and lifestyles. As explored in Chapter 5, professionalism is fundamentally structured by the customer-focused nature of transnational call center work. In the context of social, economic, and historical inequalities, the professionalism of Indian call center workers also involves performing emotional labor to make sense of and manage customer expressions of racism.

5

“Don’t Take Calls, Make Contact!”

Legitimizing Racist Abuse

In an article published in the *Harvard Business Review* a leading consultant provides the following advice to call center operators: “Don’t take calls, make contact.”[1] This is exactly the requirement placed on Indian customer service agents who are required to make “contact” despite their construction as strange and distant job thieves (as discussed in Chapters 2 and 3). This contact is achieved through an elaborate output of emotional labor that is an integral part of all service work. Both male and female Indian customer service workers are required to perform acts traditionally associated with femininity as a routine part of their jobs. At the same time, this emotion work is situated within discourses of nationalism and ethnicity. Aggressive and abusive behavior is normalized in the context of encounters between Westerners and Indians, which provide a forum for a continual process of racialization. The West is legitimized through constructions of Indians as “other” in a dynamic that parallels Robert Miles’s description of European explorers who used skin color to define Africans as “black” and, as a result, differentiated themselves in terms of skin color as well. In that context, "black" and "white" "were bound together, each giving meaning to the other."[2] Westerners and Indians are continually defining and constructing one another during service calls in racialized ways, although workers and customers occupy vastly different positions in terms of their ability to express their views to one another. In their descriptions of customers, Indian workers not only reinforce a racialized hierarchy between Westerners and Indians, but more specifically suggest that Americanness/Britishness forms a particular kind of whiteness in the context of the Western dominance of transnational subcontracting. This whiteness is characterized as hypermasculine, aggressive, and adversarial.[3] As a result, encounters of rudeness and aggression are normalized through relations of production that simultaneously situate clients as whites, as Westerners, and as customers. Customers construct Indians as servers who are required to deal with abuse *as part of their jobs.* In the context of neoliberalism and the accompanying valorization of the individual's right to free speech, customer racism is recast as an expression of product preference. It is treated as a legitimate form of customer feedback by managers, trainers, and sometimes even workers themselves.[4] Indians are racially constructed as holding a labor market position in the global economy that demands that they develop the skills needed to deal with customers' racialized aggression.

Feminized Emotion Work

The transnationalization of service jobs marks a significant departure in the ways in which gender is enacted compared to the subcontracting of manufacturing and assembly jobs. One of the hallmarks of transnational subcontracted manufacturing work has been the vast numbers of jobs specifically targeted for women workers. Since the 1970s, researchers have noted women's overrepresentation in export-processing industries.[5] Aihwa Ong argues that "if we look at the figures for all off-shore industries, women tend to comprise the lower-paid half of the total industrial work force in developing countries. . . . [T]hey are concentrated in a few industries: textiles, apparel, electronics, and footwear."[6] Women's appropriateness for these jobs is often defined in ideological terms (such as natural dexterity or assumed nimbleness), and women workers earn between 30 and 40 percent less than men worldwide.[7] As Amrita Basu and colleagues summarize, "capitalism [has] depended on sexism in order to be global."[8]

More recently, feminists writing about transnational global regimes have noted the growing *de*segregation of traditionally feminized subcontracted jobs. Meera Nanda, for example, provides evidence of the rising defeminization of offshore work by arguing that "computer-aided manufacture and flexible production techniques are changing the skill requirements and gender composition of workers employed by the apparel and microelectronics industries." Nanda also notes that women face the risk of being displaced from the export-oriented sector as men fill the requirements for better and more skilled jobs.[9] This trend of the entry of men into traditionally female-dominated service sectors is clearly evident in customer service work in India. Transnational customer service work is not a female-dominated profession, even at the entry level.[10] Both women and men are involved in call center work, and the workforce is much more stratified in terms of age and class (most workers tend to be urban, middle-class youth) than gender.

While men may be gaining predominance in traditionally female-dominated service, this does not automatically signal the decline in the requirements that service jobs require performances of conventional notions of femininity. Traditionally, service work is assumed to require specific gender enactments, which, in turn, reinforce the notion that gender differences are natural. The gender "subtext"[11] in jobs facilitates the segregation of men into positions of authority and leadership, and women into lower-paid clerical and service. With the growth of precarious employment in the West and transnational subcontracting in developing countries, assumptions regarding masculinity and femininity inherent in jobs have become far from static. Gender is embedded in jobs in the sense that these jobs are structured to require certain ways of working for all employees. As Lisa Adkins notes, "workers may perform, mobilize, and contest masculinity, femininity, and new gender hybrids in a variety of ways in order to innovate and succeed in flexible corporations. Thus men may perform (and indeed be rewarded for performing) traditional acts of femininity... and women may perform (and also be rewarded for) traditional acts of masculinity."[12] Masculinities structure Indian customer service jobs through the construction of ideal workers as entrepreneurial and competitive (as described in Chapter 4). Work also assumes a highly masculinized notion of time (to be discussed in Chapter 6). In their actual dealings with customers, however, agents are required to embody the traits that characterize highly feminized sectors such as clerical or domestic work.

While early feminist theorists focused on "women's work" as a descriptive term to refer to occupational sex segregation (or the sex of the worker in a particular job), Lisa Adkins and Eeva Jokinen observe that more recent understandings of gendered work highlight assumptions of gender ideals automatically implicit in certain jobs—"to be feminized means to be made extremely vulnerable; able to be disassembled, reassembled, exploited as a reserve labor force, seen less as workers than as servers."[13] In the context of contemporary capitalism, these exploitative work conditions pervade in many jobs occupied by both women and men. Leslie Salzinger characterizes this as "productive femininity," whereby femininity forms "a structure of meaning through which workers, potential and actual, are addressed and understood, and around which production itself is designed."[14] Rather than automatically connected to female bodies, femininity is reconstituted "as a set of transferable characteristics, including cheapness, natural docility, dexterity, and tolerance of boredom."[15]

The call center sector in India is one example of a site where notions of femininity structures the nature of work for both female and male workers. Call center operators are required to speak in ways that are symbolically coded as feminine. They are asked to be emotionally expressive and to smile while they speak on the phone. Drawing on research showing that women are more likely to be constructed as deviant for not smiling in public settings and that leadership is frequently defined in opposition to emotionality, Deborah Cameron summarizes that there are "strong symbolic links between smiling, femininity and subordinate status."[16] Workers enact femininity in Indian call centers not only by smiling while they are on the phone but also through other forms of emotion work.

The term *emotion work* has been used to describe the often invisible dimensions of the relational work that people do while caring for their families or performing their paid jobs. The literature on emotion work in paid jobs has focused considerable attention on the differences in the types of "feeling work" that individuals do in a wide variety of jobs, as well as on the expectations and norms surrounding their work.[17] Examples include managing one's own feelings on the job, making others feel a certain way, and giving definition to one's work.[18] While there has been some research on the emotion work required of workers to deal with gender and race inequality, little is known about the work done by employees when their jobs involve cross-border interactions.

Jobs also do not uniformly require such enactments of emotion work, and highly paid professional workers often have more leeway in the nature of their emotion work. Call center workers, however, are part of the "service proletariat."[19] They occupy a subservient position in relation to their customers and have little control over their emotion work. Not only are these workers required to sound a particular way, but they are also asked to manage their own emotions to ensure that they come across as familiar, caring, compassionate, and deferential, even in the face of abusive customers. Jeff Hearn terms this globalization of emotion work as the creation of "transpatriarchies": "just as there are internal sexual divisions of labor, so too there are international emotional divisions of labor."[20] These international divisions of labor are enacted on a daily basis through calls between Indian customer service agents and Western customers. Call center workers are taught to perform two kinds of "emotion work"—caring and servitude—during training programs and on the job in order to successfully provide customer service. They also manage their own emotions in light of the racism they often experience on calls. During service encounters, Indian customer service workers sometimes construct Westerners as childlike and starved of care.

Caring through Servitude

The quintessential form of women's work, according to Drucilla Barker and Susan Feiner, is "caring labor—attending to the physical and emotional needs of others."[21] They probe the relationship among care, femininity, and value through questions about who is entitled to be cared for and who is expected to care. The assumed entitlement of Western customers for care and requirement of Indian workers to care is the emotional arrangement within transnational service work. Caring, even for abusive customers, is seen as an integral part of the job. This caring involves not only listening carefully to customer needs but also providing information in ways that boost customer self-confidence. The ideal customer service agent is "someone who has a natural knack of being a people's person and can build a quick rapport and create a warm, soothing feeling."[22] Accordingly, call center operators are required to be empathetic about any problems raised by customers. One woman describes a typical call: "The caller calls up and says, 'uh, I'm very upset today. I've had a fight with my wife and this, this, this problem.' Then empathize with him. 'OK, sorry Sir, I really understand whatever you are facing. If I would have been in your position, I would have felt the same. I'm so sorry, Sir'... make him feel confident. It's not a terrible problem, and you haven't done anything wrong.... You need to apologize... 'I'm so sorry this has happened. I'm really sorry'... We have to be patient, more and more patient." A male agent similarly highlights the importance of empathy: "If they're facing some problem... you say, 'yes, I can really understand that you are being frustrated by this stuff.' Once you tell them, 'yes, I can understand, I can be in your shoes'... they're relaxed that, yes, at least, this fellow knows how painful it is, how frustrating it is to deal with such kind of hell."

The caring work performed by call center workers is accompanied by a complete deference to the authority of the customer. In general, both female and male call center workers are expected to practice servitude. A male worker, for example, notes, "You have to be empathetic. You have to be polite. Even if you are very frustrated. You cannot express your feelings to the customer.... Even if the customer shouts at you, uses abusive language. You have to be polite." Another worker similarly normalizes abusive situations: "Irate [customers] are the most difficult ones because they'll start with the four-letter words and they'll end up with a four-letter word... and it's your job to make them cool."

Emotion work in the context of customer service work involves managing customer anger. Customer service workers around the world deal with abusive customers, particularly those attempting to solve complex customer problems through short telephone interactions. The bureaucratic structure of service interactions is often frustrating and unsatisfying for customers.[23] As Winifred Poster observes, however, "what differentiates the hostility in Indian call centers versus other interactive service settings is the comments that are explicitly racial in character."[24] The assumption that agents need to recast racist and abusive interactions as part of their jobs is situated within the broader context of international competition for subcontracted customer service work. Through training curricula, media messages, and organizational processes, Indian workers are given the task of performing servitude as a way of protecting the customer service industry in India and thus performing a service to their nation.

In this way, customer abuse and the requirement for servitude is contextualized in terms of a rhetoric of national responsibility. India's attractiveness as a location for subcontracting is said to depend on workers' ability to satisfy the demands of foreign clients. Workers are encouraged to recast their servitude as an exercise in nationalism since they are performing their national duty by encouraging outsourcing. One man points to the fact that Indian workers have to ensure that they do not receive any complaints by noting, "In case you find a customer who is very difficult, even then you cannot disconnect the call.... The customer was warning me, 'if you disconnect the call, I will surely go and complain to [the American company].'" Another worker provides the following example of her display of nationalist servitude: "[In our center, customers] are calling us. But... they are of the opinion that they're calling back [the foreign company,] but that company's calls are actually diverted to our place.... So we have to be double cautious that we actually don't irritate the customer, and we have [to] serve them." Indeed, workers note that they are frequently reminded by managers and customers that their jobs could be shifted instantaneously to other countries or organizations. This serves to reinforce the notion that workers hold responsibility for events that are largely decided in corporate boardrooms in the West.[25] Joan Acker argues this "transnational business masculinity" is an example of the institutionalization of violence: "[T]he violence of leaving people without resources for survival through downsizing or moving production... is simply business necessity."[26] The rhetoric of business necessity is far from neutral when the necessity at play is that both female and male employees in another nation risk job loss if they do not fulfill the requirements of servitude and care for customers in the West.

Service workers are required to be both customer oriented and bureaucratically efficient. The logic of bureaucratization prompts organizations to rationalize processes and streamline work to reduce costs and increase efficiency. At the same time, customer orientation requires a responsive and flexible approach so that the broad range of customer needs can be satisfied. Marek Korczynski and Ursula Ott summarize that management reconciles the dual logics of customer orientation and organizational efficiency by promoting the "myth of customer sovereignty." While the customer is led to believe that he/she is the most important actor in the service interaction, the production process itself fundamentally structures the exchange. The service worker's job is to guide the customer through the constraints posed by the way in which the production process is set up.[27]

In call centers, for example, workers are often required to follow predefined protocols that limit possible customer responses. Workers often use menus to provide customers with choices from pre-established lists. When the customer experiences the limits of the service provision, which happens often, dissatisfaction leads to racialized violence. This violence is normalized by managers and trainers as being a part of the customer service agents' jobs and related to deficiencies in workers' skills. One trainer summarizes the link among racism, language, and skill: "[T]here used to be people who were very weak and they used to have a lot of regional accent. As long as you satisfy your customer with whatever queries they have, they do not have a problem wherever in the world they are calling, but if the customer is not able to follow the question, or if the person is not able to satisfy their questions or queries then they used to get really mad at us."

Strategies for managing abusive customers are conceptualized as skills to be acquired by individual workers and are taught during training programs and through on-the-job learning. In their discussions of customer abuse, however, workers construct their Western customers as hyperaggressive, unlike Indians:

> We do come across people who do abuse us a lot, for us if people do abuse us, we have to give them warning, and then we can actually drop the call. That is one thing we can do, okay, we are working in call centers, and means somebody just abuses you. Otherwise we can't drop the call, we have to deal with it. But yes, if the person gets into an argument or he starts abusing, because they do abuse a lot. Girls they cry, they cry on the floor, and we have to tell them, "don't take it so personally." It's like, it's just like you calling up your mobile company and you are not happy. Something was supposed to be done which they didn't do, naturally you are not happy, and are screaming at them. It's just that in India, we don't abuse but for them, they do.

> We don't argue back. Arguing back is a strict no, no. We can't say anything to the customer.... We have been told so many times during our training that you have to keep cool, you have to keep cool, that it actually tends to brainwash your brain, drill your brain with that sentence. So we have to keep cool, and we have to understand that they are just our customers, the people who don't

know anything. We are programmed to function in such a way, during the whole training period everyone will say that you have to keep cool, and that they are not abusing you, they are just abusing the company, things like that.

Training programs reinforce the notion of abuse as a routine part of jobs. This normalization of abuse is a form of "depersonalized bullying" whereby organizational practices support the aggressive behaviors of managers and customers.[28] One respondent, for example, shared the notes she took during her training. Alongside pages of handwritten sentences specifying "correct" responses to customer queries, there were extensive doodles (suggesting boredom) and an image that captures the abusive relationship between customer and worker.

During training, workers are told that they should expect abusive and racist comments from customers and given strategies to appease callers.

Training for Abuse. Drawing provided by respondent.

For example, the behavior of abusive callers is implicitly sanctioned since workers must provide three warnings before disconnecting a call. Marek Korczynski and Vickie Bishop argue that abuse is also sanctioned in customer service settings through the use of the term "challenging customer" rather than "violent customer."[29] In the Indian context, the term "irate" is uniformly used to refer to violent customers—a term that is not part of everyday language usage but seems to have been regularized specifically for this industry. In this context, workers are often encouraged to hold themselves responsible for irate customers because managing abuse is considered part of the entrepreneurism required for good performance on the job. One worker rationalizes customer abuse, saying, "If an agent of my level had given wrong information and it has affected a lot to that customer, so calling the next time, it will not go to that same agent. So without thinking if he starts scolding us, uses abuse. So first we have to understand exactly what the problem is." Another worker highlights the transferrable skills she has developed as a result of abusive customers: "If someone starts shouting on the other end, I used to just hang up the phone. But [here] I was taught that this is not the way you need to do it. Even if you go anywhere, you would find people who are irritated. So you need not run away from things. You need not run away from challenges. You need not run away from problems. You need to face problems." Not running away does not involve challenging abusive behavior but instead responding ironically with respect: "You have to understand, apologize. Calming him down and then give respect. So when he gets respect...if someone understands his feelings then somebody is listening to you, he'll also feel very happy because someone is interested. He's just blowing off."

Facing the problem of abusive customers is also said to require "listening skills"—this reference to skill discourse further neutralizes violence and constructs it as a job requirement just like any other job expectation such as strong communication skills, technical proficiency, or knowledge of specific processes. One worker refers to this skill: "I had customers who at the beginning of the call, they start with the slangs [abusive words]. I make them calm down. Convince them I can do their job...that's when they come into the same frequency, wherein you can communicate very easily. It's the way you put the customer across. It's the way you talk.... So it's just building confidence." Listening skills involve allowing customers to express themselves in any way they like, as one worker notes:

> One thing that I learnt from one of the people [trainers] is "listen." Understand. Genuinely listen. Understand what they are trying to say, point they are trying to make. Don't interrupt them and let them have their heart out. Once a person's heart is out, he does not have anything more to say. That is the time when he is plain, and that's the time when you pour. So after they say everything, I hear what they are trying to say. I acknowledge that he has better knowledge, and I have learnt a lot of things from him. That makes him feel better.

Customer sovereignty is closely tied to sexism. Vickie Bishop, Marek Korczynski, and Laurie Cohen argue that "in the same way as the dominance of masculine norms in organizations can make male-female violence invisible in organizations, so it may be that the ideology of customer sovereignty can operate to make customer-worker violence invisible in service organizations."[30] Customer sovereignty not only requires workers to perform the highly feminized roles of caring and servitude as part of their jobs[31] but also bolsters the sexist entrenchment of gender stereotypes. For example, the ability to empathize is often talked about as more accessible to female call center workers. One woman notes, "For females, especially for Indian females, it's okay because they're very patient, and for males... once the customer is really annoyed, you know, they have to control their ego to tell them, 'no, I'm not irritated at all.'" Another respondent explains her approach to good customer service as follows: "If he [the customer] is irate... at first, be calm and listen to him. Let him take out their anger. Let them be calm, and once they finish... 'Sorry for whatever problem you faced'... I have that ability... Boys, most of them are short tempered. They can't do as much."

Workers also perform gendered forms of emotion work in response to constructions of professionalism in call center work, which is manifest in the ability to prioritize work over personal needs and respond to job pressures with dignity.[32] Workers develop strategies to connect with customers by highlighting the uneven power held by customers and workers. One woman shares her response to angry customers: "I don't know how to convince people and tell them that I'm not going to harm you even if I tried. And some [of them] are so skeptical about giving information, I say 'Okay, if you don't trust me, here's my name, here's my employee [ID], here's where I work, so if anything goes wrong, please feel free to catch me.' That's the only way I can tell them." Workers use their lack of power to build trust and empathy: "You know, trust me, there's no other way. I want to tell them, 'What is it you have to lose?' We end up losing the job [if I cheat you]. We end up losing so many more things. So I feel integrity is very important.... I don't know how to help such people, but the only way I can help them is 'here's what you need, if you feel that you've been cheated this is enough for you to get me into trouble.' I tell them that. I even give them my supervisor's name."

Cameron Macdonald and David Merrill observe that customer service orientation both reproduces and creates systemic inequalities because customers show marked preferences for workers who look and sound a particular way. In a hardware store, for example, male service providers are assumed to be more knowledgeable about heavy equipment and tools, and female salespeople about paints and carpets. African American men are assumed to lack nurturing and soft skills. Such expectations fundamentally shape customer satisfaction or dissatisfaction with the service provided. In this way, "employers and service recipients translate race and ethnic markers into indicators of the nature of the service itself."[33] Similarly, Korczynski and Bishop cite overlaps between the ideologies of customer sovereignty and the ideologies of patriarchy, both of which normalize harassment as a normal part of "what men do."[34] Existing sexist and racist stereotypes are often used to serve organizational ends. Accordingly, women customer service workers in India note that they often experience explicit sexualized and eroticized responses from Western clients. They handle these situations by ignoring sexualized behaviors or by capitalizing on Orientalist stereotypes to complete their work. One woman reports that "When they hear a very sweet voice over the phone, they tend to flirt us... I will be coming to India next week. I would like to meet you." Another woman characterizes callers as lonely men who prefer to make free customer service calls rather than paying to call a sex line: "We have people calling in the middle of the night, drunk, troubling some of the agents. 'Why don't you come on a date.' This is not a chat center." These comments generate fear and discomfort for workers: "There was a guy from New York. [He said], 'you have a sweet voice.'... He could tell me how I look, and I was shocked. I was scared for a while, you know, this guy can't see me. I was like, does he have a camera or something? ... [H]ow can he tell me what's the color of my face? ... [He said], 'Why don't you come to New York, you sound so nice, give me your email ID... What's your cell phone number?'... And I said, 'I'm sorry, I'm not allowed to give you that.'"

Overall, behaviors that would constitute sexual harassment in face-to-face customer interactions are normalized as a natural part of phone-based customer service work. One male agent describes customer responses by arguing that it is easier for women to complete transactions: "As soon as they [customers] receive a guy, they hang up the call. When they speak to a girl, they speak, 'Where are you calling from? Are you calling from India? Oh, how is India? I've been to India two years ago.' [She says] 'Sir, can you please tell me... I'll just ask you a few questions.'"

Polite silence is expected from agents not only in the face of overt sexism but also in response to the explicitly racist behavior displayed by clients. One woman working for a lost baggage process, for example, notes that customers are justified in being angry because their vacations are often ruined when their baggage is lost and they need a forum to vent their anger. She recounts her experience with a customer who hung up on her by explaining how this incident negatively impacted on her performance scores: "[Customers] can taunt you, like, 'You Indians, you cannot do this. Bloody Indians'.... She was so frustrated she just hanged up. And that was a toll on my performance. Because I was not able to take the call properly." Another respondent recounts being called an "Indian screwer" and summarizes, "they don't take the people in India as human beings mostly. They don't treat them as human beings. They say that the Indians are like down market or something like that. They have that idea in their mind... that in India, the people are like, maybe uneducated, don't know how to deal with the people."

While customers enjoy anonymity in making these statements, workers do not, contributing to the "asymmetrical grammar"[35] that supports violence in customer service settings. As an example of this power imbalance, one worker recounts: "Sometimes they say, 'I'll sue you. I'll come to India and I'll complain against you. I'll complain to your supervisor. I'll complain to your operations manager.' So sometimes, even if you're giving the right information, you're trying to apologize, you're trying your level best... the aggression won't come out.... If you get arrogant with them, then obviously they will file a complaint against you."

This expression of customer prejudice as a legitimate expression of individual preference is characteristic of neoliberal racism. It involves the "curtailing off of the racial from the public domain...and restricting it to the privacy of occasional individual choice."[36] This privatization of racism occurs in the context of the construction of states described by David Goldberg as "traffic cops" primarily in charge of ensuring the free flow of capital and people rather than the enforcement of international labor regulations. In the name of expressing their "customer preference," Western consumers practice border enforcement through their overtly nationalist racism much like the activities of vigilante border patrol groups in the United States who privately take on the role of protecting American sovereignty with slogans such as "This is America, get off my property." Transnational service work provides the forum for the exercise of "everyday racism"[37] where Westerners can express their frustration with their own poor job prospects by telling Indians to get out of their jobs. Westerners are characterized as rude, inherently abusive, and angry; one worker notes that "some frustrated customers, they don't even want to speak to your supervisor....They will be speaking to you only but keeping on, you know, just shouting, shouting, shouting." With the privatization of racism, customers are completely immune from legislative sanction.

Saving Face

Despite the strong directive to care, management control over workers' emotion work is far from complete. The complexity of customer service work also allows for the possibility of worker empowerment since management cannot fully dictate customer responses or worker feelings.[38] Workers are acutely aware of the imperative to act as though they care. While they experience customer abuse as highly stressful, they do not talk about being estranged from themselves. Rather, they construct the requirement to show they care as an instrumental job requirement. The empathy deemed necessary as a key component of customer service work is often displayed by Indian workers in the context of a culture of antipathy. In general, antipathy is generated by the communal construction of Western customers through a negative lens. Korczynski and Bishop note that antipathy can be a preemptive strategy for coping with abusive customers. This is the contradictory experience of service work where customers are experienced simultaneously as "friend and enemy."[39] When empathy temporarily reigns, workers recount instances of connection:

> Most of the time they [customers calling to make purchases from the catalogue] are very old people who are not able to shop or even walk as well. There were sometimes people who have just been discharged from hospitals... they need a kind of dress and they are not even able to shop. There were times when people have told me their own feelings and own personal problems, and I also cried for that. One of the calls, I still remember, this old man called up. He wanted a trouser and a shirt. He bought it and he said, "Do pray for me". I said "I will pray for you." I forgot his name. Then he said, "Do you know the reason why I asked you to pray?" I said "no." He said "I am suffering from leukemia." I said, "I'm so sorry."

> She [the customer] was just going on as if there was nobody with who she can talk. She's pouring everything into me. I said, "OK, let me listen." She was so glad that at the end of the call, she said: "Why don't you come and have Christmas dinner with me?" So I said, "I'm sorry but you're calling in India." She said, "Whenever you come here, you just come to my place" and gave me her address.... That gives me satisfaction, OK, I spoke to a lady who was very elderly, of my mother's age, and I built up a relationship with her.... She wanted me to call her Granny. She didn't feel she called a call center. She feels she called someone she knows.

These instances of connection do not, however, translate into positive performance scores for workers. Agents recount dozens of incidents when their average handling time or customer satisfaction scores are dependant less on their performance than on customer idiosyncrasies. While workers' time is scrutinized, the structure of work places no constraints on customers' time. One woman recounts, "There it's midnight so customers who are a little drunk, they call for nothing.... They just won't keep the phone down, and you are not allowed to disconnect.... The problem is with people who are drunk and who don't use profanity, they just keep babbling around, nothing to the point, and we can't disconnect the phone. Because that would go against us, straight zero on the call. 45 minutes, 50 minutes, we have to take calls whereas our average handling time is 5 minutes. So that one call takes our statistics for a toss." Workers have little recourse when faced with such customers: "There are times when I have [been] just listening to the customer for 17 minutes, 20 minutes, just listen. If he is irate, keep aside your AHT [average handling time]...because you would not feel good to transfer the call to your supervisor hundred time. Ten times a day, call to supervisor...he will get frustrated and irate doing that constant." Performance measures also ignore customer nationalism: "Even if you do resolve the issue, the customer still knows that you are from India and the accent does matter there. So although the issue is resolved they send [a feedback score of] 3 or 2 (out of 5). It's kind of irritating for us to take that because on the call they will be very happy. You worked hard, you resolved my issue, and finally they give you 3 or 2 out of 5. So it's kind of disappointing at that point of time." As demonstrated by the comments above, workers note the inconsistency between the managerial performance criteria and the erratic customers who undermine the accuracy of these same measures. At times, workers construct Westerners as being in need of therapy:

> This one time, I was on a call, and there was this lady, and I couldn't pronounce her surname. She was American, and she said, you know, "What difference does it make, I'm getting divorced." I said, "I'm very sorry," you know, because I didn't know what to say. She said, "Oh, don't be sorry, I've had twelve years of a disastrous marriage, and I don't know what to do. I've to start from scratch, all over again." And, you know, I told her, "There are so many things you can do, move on with your life, get a job, get a post."...So, then I just made a little joke: "You want to know what, you're speaking to somebody who is miles away, and it's two a.m. in the morning and I'm still talking to you." So then she started laughing. So at the end of the day, she did put the phone down, but she was really happy...by the time she was done with me she was actually giggling.

Customers' personal revelations are sometimes characterized as a pathological form of overfamiliarity. An agent recounts, "I remember one old lady. She was really good. It's just that she was alone. She didn't have kids, and she met an accident. She lost her leg.... We spoke a lot. Then she said, 'Hey, baby, why don't you come down here [to the U.S.].' I mean they are so attached to you once they speak to you. 'Why don't you come here and stay with me.' I was like, 'Oh, what!' How can she do that? I mean she doesn't know me."

In the context of these experiences, workers develop perspectives on cultural differences between Indians and Westerners; as one worker notes,

"American client, he'll say, 'What the hell are you doing?'...For us, it's a very big thing, what this person has said, we really take it to heart. But out there, it's just a common thing. It's that way." These highly stereotypical "cultural" constructions of Western cultures are overtly reinforced in training materials. One training manual has a section entitled "Appreciating Western Culture," which contains a summary of American and British "characteristics": "people from the United Kingdom are generally: conservative and class conscious, reserved, law abiding and principled, ethnocentrically arrogant, conscious about time." The following are some of the basic traits of Americans and the rules governing their social and family relationships: appreciate equal opportunity, forthright, informal, independent, materialistic, value time, sensitive to gender and diversity issues.[40]

Bishop, Korczynski, and Cohen note that workers develop several strategies to cope with abusive customers. They put on a brave face, rationalize abuse by citing examples of inefficient co-workers, swap stories, and form communities of coping.[41] In transnational service situations, workers also evoke nationalist and racist stereotypes to normalize abusive responses from customers, and construct servitude and caring as part of their jobs. By using stereotypes to refer to their customers, Indian service providers disrupt hierarchies of class and nation between them and their Western customers. Identities and cultures are thus constructed, negotiated, and given meaning in interactions between workers. As Tina Basi observes, this occurs "over and over again throughout the labor process, in an exchange with every new customer. Each customer brings his or her own understanding of what it means to be 'Indian' to the exchange and, through a dialogic process with the call center worker, constructs a new identity for the employee."[42]

As noted in Chapters 3 and 4, Indians class themselves as better educated and more skilled than their customers in the West. As India's new middle class, call center workers serve often abusive and sometimes erratic customers but are also aware of their position in the Indian society where they have the income to exercise their own customer sovereignty vis-à-vis local service providers. This class awareness is evident in the following comment when one worker recounts an interaction with an angry customer: "He actually got so frustrated, he started abusing, like 'fuck you' and all that. So I said that, 'Sir, if you use profanity then I have to hang up the phone.' Then he [said] 'OK, fine, I won't abuse. I am sorry for that.'

Even he said 'sorry!'...I had to handle it very professionally. That is the thing. The professionalism has to be there. Whether you are talking to a housewife, whether you're talking to a maid servant, but that thing has to be there."

Sharon Bolton and Maeve Houlihan observe that the current approach to customer service "squeezes the human out and undermines the process of service provision."[43] Instead, they note that customer relations should be reconceptualized as social relations free from hierarchies of servitude. These theorists note that "if the emotion work involved in providing customer service is viewed as a social accomplishment, front-line service workers can then be conceptualized as multi-skilled emotion managers who are able to expertly judge what time and how much emotion work is required to maintain a stable and mutually satisfying order of interaction."[44] Such an approach would involve proactive state and organizational strategies to disrupt the possibility that transnational call centers serve as the forum for the expression of nationalism and racism. Without such intervention, every time a public figure in the West condemns outsourcing in the name of protecting jobs in the Western labor market, individual customers' racism toward Indian agents is sanctioned. Unions, activists, and politicians all play a role in legitimizing customer anger by constructing outsourcing as job theft and failing to connect offshoring policies to local economic actors. While in most cases customers cannot walk into a local convenience store or supermarket and spew racist slurs with impunity, the absence of any labor or anti-harassment laws for voice interactions has given rise to a situation where such actions are everyday occurrences on calls.

In the context of transnational economic relations, customer service work in India clearly involves a multifaceted set of tasks through which workers can become the kinds of workers who can legitimately serve Westerners. This authenticity work of "connecting" with Western clients requires the constant management of one's own feelings and demands an inordinate amount of stamina from workers. Due to their long shifts and night work, they often perform this work in a state of physical exhaustion as will be discussed in Chapter 6. Given the synchronous nature of customer service work, agents' jobs follow Western clocks, and many of them cite their night-time shifts as the most challenging feature of their jobs.

6

Being Nowhere in the World

Synchronous Work and Gendered Time

> You are nowhere. You are not there in the world. It seems as if you are not there in the world because when the world is awake, you are asleep, and when the world is asleep, you are awake. And it is just that you go, you come, you go to sleep, you get up, you go, you come, you go to sleep, you get up, you go, you come, you go to sleep.

> When I went [for this] job, I was very jubilant. I thought, "OK, I'll study a lot, daytime is mine, so I'll be able to do anything." That's not possible. You're so tired. You're not able to do anything. Whatever time [you have] you sleep, even if you sleep for ten hours you don't get enough... you can never compensate a night's sleep.... It's taxing, it's taxing, it's taxing on your social, it's taxing on your health, it's taxing on everything.

> Actually, we are just cut off from society. We don't know what is going on. We don't know what's happening around us. Because by the time they go to sleep, we have to wake up, and when we wake up, when we are working, everybody is sleeping.

> Nothing is there. In the nighttime, no friends are there. Family members, they cannot sit with you a whole night [to] speak to you.

Such images of spatial and temporal loneliness pepper customer service agents' reflections on their work. Despite their daily virtual migrations, workers feel deeply embedded in their local, immediate, physical contexts. One of the widely cited advantages of the outsourcing of software programming to India is that work can occur around the clock. Work done at head offices in the West can be continued in offshore locations during their day so that organizations can operate continuously. Call center workers, however, do not work when their counterparts in the West are asleep. Due to the synchronous nature of customer service work and the high volume of service calls during customers' days, outsourcing to India necessitates night work. This chapter explores the social and organizational responses to the challenges posed by working at night. While most respondents cite their night work as the single greatest challenge of their jobs, work processes in call centers ignore the consequences of night work. Indeed, "time" is conceptualized in terms of "clock time"—the counting of minutes with a focus on work times and average handling times—rather than as time embedded within social relations.[1] The ways in which work time interacts with the particular material space occupied by workers is obscured by the overwhelming focus on clock time as a symbol of professionalism. In fact, workers do more than live according to the waking times of their Western customers. As the quotes at the beginning of this chapter demonstrate, workers also manage the emptiness created in the spaces from which they are temporally absent.

The Professional Clock: Work Schedules and Average Handling Times

Indian call centers are at the forefront of the confluence between geographical time and capitalist time given the time-sensitive nature of synchronous customer service work. Workers work, eat, and interact at times that exist in faraway geographies rather than according to the time rhythms of their local settings. Capitalist exchange requires such a time disjuncture because labor costs drive organizational decisions about the location of work. Barbara Adam argues that transnational corporations export Western time across the globe. They facilitate the "colonization with time," where time is a "quantifiable resource that is open to manipulation, management and control, and subject to commodification, allocation, use and abuse."[2] Time can be traded just like raw materials and labor. Such an approach that constructs time as money is based on the assumption that "capital has a built-in clock that is constantly ticking away."[3]

In call centers, time is controlled via notions of professionalism that are closely associated with the clock. Through the focus on clock time, attention is on the passage of time (log-in shifts, break times, handling times) rather than the context-specific activities that inhabit a particular time period (time for sleeping, time for going to school, time for eating). As explored in earlier chapters, notions of professionalism go hand in hand with constructions of hierarchies of backwardness and modernity in Indian call centers. This is enacted specifically in terms of frequent references to the need for Indians to learn Western approaches to "time management" reminiscent of colonial discourses of the "lazy native."[4] One manager, who served as a call center agent for several years before he was sent to the United States for training, reflects on the nature of Americans: "They are very much particular, very punctual...[and we Indians] should learn a lot from this." Another worker recounts the process of his own learning by saying, "Initially [I had a] casual attitude toward work, not coming on time. Then I realized that I was not being professional. Team leader made me realize." Time management is clearly constructed as a "skill"; as one agent reports, "I learned a lot...time management was the best thing. How to manage the time if you have twenty-four hours in a day. How...you should manage, so that you can improve."

While an often cited hallmark of professional jobs in the West is the discretion over time, professionalism in Indian call centers ironically translates into an intense scrutiny of workers' time to ensure that agents learn time norms. These norms such as punctuality and time management are presented to agents as universally superior naturalized dimensions of Western work cultures. When wages are conceptualized as payment for a workers' time, the use of time is linked to profit. This link between time and profit gives rise to work processes that are focused on an intense control of workers' schedules. In this context, workers report long working hours during which they are required to account for each minute through log-in times [times when they are at their terminals and answering or awaiting calls], times between calls and breaks. On calls, the time spent with each caller is computed and aggregated, and performance scores based on the average handling time (AHT) of each employee are produced. Much of this control of time is facilitated through automatic dialing technologies that ensure back-to-back calls. These technologies eliminate the time taken and discretion involved in manually dialed calls, and also remove any spaces between calls. These technologies designed to eliminate "idle" time lengthen real working hours.[5] Employees are monitored not only locally but also by the client firms in the West. Winifred Poster reports that "the minutia of employee call activity is directly observable by client firms in the U.S. They can view computer screens of each agent in real time, or ask the quality control department in the Indian call center to patch them through to a particular agent and listen in on the current call."[6]

Not surprisingly, this minute-to-minute monitoring translates into considerable stress for workers; as one agent notes, "[At] 8:30, I have to log in. I have to means I have to. It should not be 8:31. The pressure is there, you know, it has to be. Not a second here, it has to be dot here. That mental pressure is here. I have to log in at 8:30." Aside from the mental pressure, workers also perceive the loss of control over their times: "You're bonded. You don't have the choice. When they want you to go for lunch, you go. You don't have the free time. You cannot tell I want this shift. Even if I want to leave I have to ask."

Most workers report being given weekly, rotating work schedules. For some, the schedule changes as often as every week, and many workers have no fixed days off. Scheduled assignments also allow little room for negotiation: "There are six, seven [start] times in [my company]. Seven o'clock, ten o'clock, one o'clock, 2:30, 3:30, five, eight and nine—eight times in fact. So you can be given any shift.... You rotate per week.... Sometimes what happens is, let's say you have off on Saturday, Sunday. The next week offs follows immediately on Monday, Tuesday. So you get four weekly offs. Saturday, Sunday, Monday, Tuesday after which without any rest period you have to keep working for ten days."

Most respondents report doing a nine-hour shift, which comprises eight hours of log-in time and one hour of break. In addition, some workers have discretion over their break times, while others have assigned break times. Agents also note that break times are dependent on call flow. This flexibility is justified in terms of the "customer-focused" nature of the business: "We have to follow the schedule. Log in time. Your first break within this time. But then, if you don't take... like if you're busy on call at ten o'clock, you can't take your break. Because you can't just hang up and go for break." Clock time is therefore frequently violated when it serves organizational ends. This is constructed as a necessary flexibility for customer service work: "[The company] in these terms is very well-planned. The complete arrangement is customer-focused. Like, ideally, we have three breaks. One 30-minutes break and two 15-minutes break.... [W]hen the call flow was high, we were given three 20-minute breaks. So you could not complete your lunch. They are very customer-focused." This respondent goes on to report how workers can meet personal needs between breaks through a "break button" even though this recourse involves shortening other breaks to maintain the eight-hour log-in requirement: "You have seven minutes of extra allowance, what we call 'buy a break,' you know, washrooms.... If you are late by a minute then they calculate... your performance scores are affected. Again your incentives are affected." While there is little time flexibility for agents, break-time flexibility is frequently exercised by managers: "On Mondays, there used to be a very huge call flow. There used to be back-to-back calls. So if you log in at 5:30 p.m., the calls used to hit the floor. So we used to start taking calls.... [T]here was no break. We used to not be able to drink water also." Workers also report the common requirement of forced overtime to accommodate call flows: "Sometimes, you don't want to do a ten-hour shift when you are forced to do [it] at no extra break. You'll be getting the same three breaks, but you'll be getting a ten-hour shift."

Workers are told that since clients in the West dictate the number of agents required to be logged in at any given time, unscheduled absences have a significant impact on workgroups, particularly in the context of the existing work intensification. For this reason, any leave has to be planned in advance, and some agents report that they are forced to quit their jobs because of exams or illnesses. One worker received four unpaid leave days for his wedding, and another received nine unpaid days at the time of the birth of his child. Unplanned leave results in severe penalties in terms of performance scores and incentives, and could eventually lead to termination. Based on this situation, workers report frequently going to work sick: "[I hurt] my hand. I fell from steps. I was not able to work. The pain was unbearable. But still I don't want to be marked on my parameter because... if you just call them, OK. 'I'm not able to come to office,' then they will mark you as unplanned.... We have one thousand points as a bonus point for attendance so you will lose that.... After that for every off, you'll get INR 500 deducted from your salary.... [Y]ou can't afford to take leaves."

This exacting time and schedule discipline required of Indian customer service agents are akin to work processes at many call centers around the world. This universalization of time-management techniques at call centers, however, masks a central feature of Indian call centers: the night work. Indeed, the space of work is set up to emulate the daytime schedules of the Western customers. One worker explains the effect of this spatial set-up: "On the floor, we don't feel sleepy. Because the calls are hitting back-to-back. There the environment, there's television, there's sounds, there's songs. We don't feel sleepy. It is the day for us over there." When asked about the effect of night work on her quality scores, however, the same respondent goes on to say, "It's up and down. Sometimes when you feel sleepy... we have to ask them, 'Sorry, what did you say?' That time, the mark goes down [snaps fingers]."

Another agent recounts that workers are not allowed to even acknowledge that they are working in the middle of the night: "For the customer who is calling when you're actually logging out, that can be your last call for the day, but for the customer, it's his first call and you have to sound your best. You should not be sleepy at all." Poster argues that "virtual work in call centers does not inject agents into a 'time-less' zone where they are able to forget what time it is.... Instead, time is an even more present and immediate part of the job."[7] The focus on "clock time" allows for the enactment of work processes that obscure the social and bodily reality reported by most call center workers: that they are working at a time when they feel isolated from their families, least energetic, and most tired. These compose workers' local, embodied contexts, or "timescapes." As Adam notes, the concept of "timescape" "acknowledges that we cannot think about time separately from space and matter, that is, without embodiment in a specific and unique context."[8] The embodied experience of night work is determined to a large extent by how much sleep a worker is able to get during the daytime. This in turn is influenced by their health, involvement in their households, other work and education activities, and responsibilities to perform domestic and care work.

The "Timescape" of Night Work

Indian call centers providing service to Western customers are required to operate primarily during Western daytime hours. Although workers may at times have partial night shifts, many are assigned shifts that occur fully during the night in rotation. Based on interviews with workers in Noida and Gurgeon, Poster draws a parallel between call center agents and other migrant workers who are "pulled away from the family to serve global economies."[9] Unlike migrant workers, however, call center workers are temporally absent in the typical time rhythms of their households but are still present as household members. Not all workers experience this temporal displacement as problematic for the same reasons. Workers without household responsibilities, many of whom are young or male, primarily cite health-related impacts of night work: "The impact was like physical conditions, health conditions. Because we used to work at night, and we used to sleep in the day. It was totally against the nature. I faced a lot of problems... I faced bad ulcers, [they] used to come in my mouth." Particularly difficult are the constant shift changes:

> You need, at least, three to four hours of sleep in the night. That's what makes the big difference.... That is what is making it difficult. I'm losing my appetite, I'm losing my weight... suddenly we were told we would be having our [shift] from twelve [midnight] to eight. It was very difficult to adjust in the first few weeks. Then I got adjusted to that time. Then, again, we were told that you're having your shifts from 7:30 p.m. till 4 a.m. And this shift, I find it very difficult to adjust. That is because I get home around 7 a.m., and it's very difficult to sleep in the morning because people wake up, they go around here and there.

Workers report that they hesitate to even mention their family responsibilities at work. Their family arrangements are scrutinized during the hiring process, and marriage and children are seen as a burden. One participant brought her "appointment letter" to show me during our meeting. Her letter states that employees must provide a set of documents at the time of their appointment. This list includes the employee's marriage certificate, photographs of spouse and all children, and letters from all previous employers. Another woman reported that she was specifically asked about her marriage plans during her job interview: "They said... 'See, if you get married, what are you going to do?' I said, 'I don't have any plans for at least a year now, so cool down. I will not leave [the company].'"

Call center workers who assume some responsibility for cooking, childcare, or eldercare find night work extremely stressful. One woman with a six-year-old child recounts her schedule:

> We [she and her husband who is also employed at a call center] reach [home] at 7:30 or 8:30 a.m., then, means I don't sleep that time. I have a kid. So... means like he goes to school. So I just like help my

> mother-in-law...three or four hours go in household work, like to clean the house, wash clothes, and all....In the afternoon, I will have to sleep two or three hours. That's it...my son comes from school. So when he comes in, sometimes I have to take his homework also....After one or two years, we become irritable....Like on small issues, we get angry a lot...I am planning to now discontinue this job.

This woman was interviewed in 2007 and then again in 2009. She had continued her employment as a call center worker for financial reasons. She had, however, managed to switch to a U.K. process which allowed her to get home by 2 a.m. and spend a longer period of the night at home. In spite of her experience, her salary in 2009 was only slightly higher than in 2007. Her relatively low pay suggests that women in need of schedule flexibility compromise their salaries. Others who have household responsibilities report relying on parents or employing domestic workers. Many respondents discussed the negative impact of their night work on their parents' lives. None reported a significant shift in the gendered assignment of household responsibility. Reena Patel notes that although women gain independence and access to income through their paid work in call centers, there is little evidence that gendered divisions of household labor are changing. Instead, elderly women in the household, such as mothers and mother-in-laws, assume the role of household managers, and domestic workers are frequently hired by those who can afford this option. As a result, "under the guise of economic development and women's liberation, the bodies of elderly women are used to fuel the career aspirations of some younger women."[10] In line with this, rather than considering a gendered sharing of household responsibility, men respond by expressing a desire for a stay-at-home wife to help out. A young man explains his upcoming wedding as a household strategy to provide support for his mother: "I usually try to avoid [the] thought of my mother especially because...it's crucial for us to work and me, my brother, and my sister-in-law, all three of us are in call centers. And all three of us have different timings. For a lady who is sixty-five, and all three of us coming at different timings and opening the doors for us is really troublesome."

Despite women's economic gains, therefore, the reliance on parents and domestic helpers further entrenches the devaluation of work associated with social reproduction.[11] Indeed, as Preeti Singh and Anu Pandey's survey of one hundred female call center employees reveals, most workers were unable to balance work and family; those who were unmarried left household work to their parents and spent most of their free time sleeping due to the exhaustion associated with their night work.[12] One worker describes her routine: "I used to just come home, eat, go to sleep, go to college, that also not very regularly, get up, go to work." Based on a field study of 277 customer service agents in six call centers, Babu Ramesh summarizes that the "social frame of patriarchy...adds constraints that make it unviable for women to continue in the work for long, with odd working hours. The stress and strain at work lead to situations where the female workers cannot carry on, especially during pregnancy.... [This suggests] that BPO work is also equally or more women-unfriendly as compared to traditional manufacturing sector jobs."[13]

Women without extended families or the resources to hire domestic helpers, therefore, have two options—they can either be siphoned toward day work in call centers or leave their jobs. The centers that do have day shifts, however, employ few workers during the day. The scarcity of call center jobs during the day occurs because call volumes are much lower when most Western customers are asleep. For the day shifts, wages are lower, performance incentives do not exist, and there are no opportunities for career progression. In light of this scarcity of daytime work, most women have little choice but to leave their jobs. Therefore while women and men may enter call center employment in equal numbers, the long-term prospects for career progression for women workers is significantly hindered by the gendered allocation of household and childcare responsibilities. Many unmarried women report that their continued employment in call centers will depend largely on the sanction of their future husbands and in-laws. For workers with household responsibilities who may be allowed to work at a call center, there is little organizational accommodation of these responsibilities. As Claire Williams notes, "no one is actually rewarded for taking [time off to tend to family responsibilities]. Instead, those who demonstrate unconditional devotion to their work receive the best jobs, giving men an unfair advantage over women."[14]

Night work is gendered not only because of women's primary responsibility for domestic work and childcare but also in light of social norms. Patel argues that women working at night are treated with suspicion because the urban nightscape is seen as a male space where any women present are assumed to be engaged in sex work. Women working as call center agents continually negotiate mobility-morality norms[15] in dealing with resistance to their night work: "I have friends where I live and [they] say that people who work in BPOs are not good girls.... I have people talking of moral ethics, like people who work in BPOs coming late night... have you heard Radio Mirchi?[16] [They say] people should start wearing condoms, people working in BPOs." The historical association of night work and sex work are difficult to shake: "In Indian society, if you tell somebody that you're working in a call center, they look at you like, oh my God, because you're working at night and everybody knows the kind of people who work there. Nobody really, from the watchman to your neighbor to your parents, nobody would really respect you so much if you're working in a call center." A migrant worker shares her parents' response to her work: "In Darjeeling, people don't have a good feeling about BPOs. My mom she calls me everyday and says 'come back home, come back home.' Another woman, who is engaged to be married, talks about the difficulty of working at night, especially in the context of joint families: "[My in-laws] wouldn't want me to work in the night shift.... Living with parents, of course, that will be a problem.... If someone's coming, they'll want us to be at home.... When it's a new family you're going into, you don't [pause], and, of course, my parents will never want me to be in a call center after marriage."

Women deal with this resistance by noting the professionalism and safety of their work. Rather than challenging patriarchal family structures, fathers play an even greater role in allowing women to work in call centers given the potential impact on safety and reputation. Shelly Tara and P. Ilavarasan Vigneswara's interviews with call center workers and their parents reveal that fathers interpret transportation facilities and organizational control over work time as an indication of the organizational responsibility for women's reputation. One father interviewed for their project notes: "I allow my daughter to go to office parties only when there is transport facility by the organization but I do not send her for the parties organized by colleagues because there is nobody to take the responsibility."[17] Parental support is gained only through the transfer of responsibility from individual patriarchs (fathers) to institutional patriarchs (organizations)—women's morality and women themselves continue to be seen to need protection.

While employers acknowledge that night work poses special challenges for female workers, this recognition is addressed only through special surveillance to attempt to ensure women's bodily safety rather than any responsibility for, or recognition of, household work. Evoking a "dangerous spaces" rhetoric,[18] many call centers provide vans that pick up workers at the beginning of a shift and drop them at their homes after the completion of their shifts. This seems to be the primary, indeed, the only organizational response to night work. Constructed as a perk, van services are offered as a response to the absolute hegemony of work time expressed through rotating shifts, flexible "off" days, night work, and compulsory holiday work. These are all requirements of the call center industry. In this way, "the transnational organization of production builds non-responsibility into the structure of capitalist processes."[19] The impact of work processes and structures on households and communities are seen as private, individual concerns for which organizations assume no responsibility. Instead, organizational responsibility is limited to a worker's need to get to work on time, facilitated through the provision of vans in the context of the almost complete absence of public transportation during the night.

Significantly, since vans provide transportation to large numbers of workers, they can add up to three hours to the work time of each employee every day. Although appreciative of the service, workers also report that the structure of pick-ups and drop-offs can add considerably to their work time. One man notes, for example, that he is always the "last drop" because all the women in the cab have to be dropped off first. As a result of these circumstances, he generally spends two to three hours on the road. A woman reports the cancellation of her van service and its replacement with a shuttle bus. Rather than being picked up from her home, she is expected to go to a bus stop, which involves traveling ten minutes in an auto rickshaw in the middle of the night. For her, this change results in additional costs as well as safety concerns. Another man, who tries to sleep just prior to his shift, shares his experience with the vans: "The bad part is this cab... before one hour or two hours of the shift. For example, you have shift at around eleven o'clock [p.m.], these guys will be calling you right from 9:30, 'bhaiya bahar aajao' [please come outside]... Because what they do is if they drop someone they are in the same locality." Workers risk being denied vans for not answering their phones.

Although there is little information about the social organization of subcontracted van services, accounts of these services indicate that the drivers are on short-term contracts and held responsible for getting workers to workplaces on time. Clarifying how these services are operated, Petlee Peter describes the drivers' work schedules: "The cab drivers, who do not meet the time schedule, after being excused on a couple of occasions, are imposed a fine of INR 650 by some of the companies. On an average, a driver covers up to 450 kilometers per day."[20]

There are also incidents of violence committed by cab drivers while transporting employees. In a highly publicized case in 2008, a twenty-two-year-old IBM employee was raped by a driver on the way home from work.[21] Organizations responded by posting security guards in taxis transporting female employees. This situation, however, led to further intrusion into the women workers' nonwork time. One worker reflects on the impact of this incident: "Girls have more and more problem because once you get picked up, they call you. Once you come home, even after coming home after two, three hours, they will confirm whether you really arrived or not." Women are not allowed to leave their workplaces until both driver and security guard are available: "It's very strict. Until they get a security, we cannot sit in the cab. If sometimes the cab driver comes without security, we have to make them go back and come back. So it becomes like two, three hours late."

Higher than usual salary structures, van services, and the construction of the call center work as professional allow some women to challenge the resistance to their night work that they encounter from family and friends. At the same time, as Patel summarizes, "although the presence of middle-class women in the urban nightscape represents a break in traditional norms, their mobility and spatial access is based on regimes of control and surveillance."[22] In this context, organizations control when and how women leave their homes and workplaces, while women feel they constantly need to justify the nature of their employment.

Van services represent the sum total of organizational accommodation made in response to night work. Working at night is normalized by organizations as a "business requirement." Time is constructed as a naturalized job requirement, and a necessary dimension of synchronous transnational customer service work—after all, one can hardly expect customer service lines to be open only during customers' nights. However, there is little recognition that night work necessitates temporal autonomy and more control over breaks to compensate for the bodily effects of night work.[23] Rather than minimizing the effects of night work, the focus remains on the inevitability of night work in transnational call centers.

While David Harvey argues that one of the central features of global capitalism is "time-space compression,"[24] where space is annihilated by time, the experiences of call center workers suggest an opposite trend. Instead, they experience "time-space expansion"[25] as workers are detached from the spaces of social life such as markets, households, and transportation facilities, all of which occur during the day. While there are tax shelters, legislative amendments, and infrastructure investment directed toward attracting transnational entrepreneurs to establish call centers in India, no state resources are directed toward helping workers employed in these jobs.[26] As a result, no nighttime services exist to support call center workers; daycares, schools, hospitals, markets, public transport, governmental offices, and bill-paying facilities continue to operate as though night workers do not exist. Although women workers are the most affected by these trends given the gendered division of household labor, this generalized lack of support also affects male employees who may be involved in the care of their parents and families and embedded in social networks outside work.

The issue of time poses one of the most significant challenges in the transnationalization of service work. Becoming closer to the West in time without being closer geographically demands a monumental shift not only for transnational service workers themselves but also for all those with whom their lives are intertwined. Ursula Huws notes, for example, that, "the interpenetration of time zones in one sphere of life leads inexorably to the development of a twenty-four-hour economy as people forced to work non-traditional hours then need to satisfy their needs as consumers during abnormal times, which in turn obliges another group to be on duty to provide these services, ratcheting up a process whereby opening hours are slowly extended right across the economy, and with them the expectation that it is normal for everything always to be open."[27] This work-time complexity epitomizes the global trend of the increased participation of women in paid work accompanied by a shockingly static gendered division of responsibility for social reproduction and household work. One worker who was extremely successful in her call center job and quick to climb the organizational hierarchy quit her job immediately after her marriage. Although her husband was supportive of her employment, her mother-in-law, who was living in a different city, found it unacceptable that her son would have to come home and heat his dinner up by himself. She insisted that her daughter-in-law seek daytime employment.

Lisa Adkins notes a major shift in recent decades whereby "women's relationship to their labor is no longer governed by a logic of male-female exchange in the private sphere."[28] Contemporary women, like men, are expected to be engaged in paid employment, and being a good mother involves providing economically in addition to being there to care for their families. For call center workers, the absolute incompatibility of work time and family time leaves only one option—the outsourcing of family care to others. This strategy, which is open only to those who can afford it, magnifies the separation of paid and unpaid labor, and further entrenches the devaluation of household and care work. Women and men employed in call centers develop individual strategies in the context of the "discursive gymnastics"[29] through which transnational subcontracted IT-related work is presented by managers as gender neutral while they ignore the issue of time and responsibility for social reproduction. At the same time, women workers confront rigid expectations that they should take on 90 percent of the domestic and household work.[30] For these workers, the twenty-four-hour economy requires the superhuman feat of working for transnational organizations during the night and being there for families during the day.

CONCLUSION

Authenticity Work in the Transnational Service Economy

The focus on authenticity work highlights the proactive, conscious, and continual negotiation of sameness and difference that is the bedrock of the transnational service economy. This work is largely invisible and rarely spoken about. It is closely related to dimensions of work that theorists have referred to as invisible work, emotion work, tailoring work, immaterial labor, bodywork, interpretive work, caring work, and aesthetic labor.[1] I argue, however, that the term *authenticity work* highlights an important dimension that is thus far underexplored—the work of establishing legitimacy in the context of colonial histories and transnational economic relations. As the chapters in this book have highlighted, for Indian customer service workers, being authentic requires them to be simultaneously similar and different from their Western customers. In the transnational call center sector, this negotiation occurs on a minute-to-minute basis as hundreds of thousands of Indian agents interact directly with masses of Western customers.

Based on their study of cell centers in seventeen countries, Rosemary Batt and her colleagues note that "language and culture constrain the locational choices of corporations, creating a pattern of offshoring that differs substantially from that found in manufacturing, where cost and access to markets are primary drivers."[2] Indeed, in voice-to-voice interactions, customers and workers "hear" and construct one anothers' language and culture continually. Part of the job of customer service agents working for organizations who face global competition for offshoring contracts is to establish their legitimacy and be heard as ideal transnational service workers. While this book has explored the authenticity work of customer service workers in India, not all transnational call center workers perform the same kinds of authenticity work. For example, one-third of Canadian call centers serve U.S. clients.[3] Immigrants, women, and youth working at these centers establish their legitimacy in significantly different ways than their counterparts working in offshore jobs in India. They may construct themselves as model immigrants or responsible youth and interact with U.S. customers accordingly. Transnational domestic workers or nurses may similarly do the work of reading ideal notions of caring, and construct themselves as workers best placed to provide such care given their own national histories. The transnationalization of any kind of service work requires the negotiation of the national borders that are being crossed, and this negotiation occurs as part of service interactions. In this sense, all workers involved in providing service transnationally perform authenticity work, although the actual nature of this work differs according to the nature of the work and the border being crossed. Focusing on authenticity work allows a glimpse into the iterative nature of the local and global as transnational interactions are structured by highly localized histories which, in turn, are differently evoked by various actors. A large part of authenticity work is invisible and individualized, although consequences for failing to correctly read the imagined ideal or emulate the traits of this worker are severe. This is because, like most other service workers, call center agents experience the gaping hole in regulatory entitlements in the context of contemporary neoliberalism. Authenticity work represents employees' attempts to manage and challenge these trends, while simultaneously establishing their legitimacy as ideal transnational service workers. In India, this work occurs in the context of colonial histories, state policies, class structures, and transnational capital flows.

Becoming the Authentic Global Worker

The word *authenticity* is ordinarily used to signify something that is real or original.[4] Indeed, authenticity continues to be a widespread contemporary mechanism for the assignment of value—the authentic is that which is real, true, and genuine. Artists, musicians, and performers frequently market their products through claims of authenticity. Australian online aboriginal art dealer, Artlandish,[5] for example, provides customers with a "guarantee of authenticity" that includes the artist's name, a detailed profile of his or her life story, and a photograph of the artist while she/he is in the process of producing the work. Authenticity, therefore, does not reside in a painting but rather in the aboriginal artist—authentic aboriginal art is produced by aboriginal artists. But who is positioned to claim, or assess claims of, aboriginality? Claims of authenticity involve the establishment and recognition of the social location of actors. Establishing the "real" involves making a normative judgment. Authenticity is often claimed through ethnic or cultural identity.[6] In constructing their work as authentic, for example, artists claim the status to represent and speak about the group of which they name themselves as members. Authenticity claims, however, are not only made but also received and evaluated by socially located groups and individuals, such as artists, marketers, and customers, who come to sometimes opposing conclusions about what is "real" and "fake." As Richard Peterson notes, "authenticity is a claim that is made by or for someone, thing, or performance and either accepted or rejected by relevant others."[7] The effort involved in claiming self-legitimacy is *authenticity work*.

Authenticity work occurs continually through interactions. As Jabar Gubrium and James Holstein summarize, "issues of authenticity infuse all aspects of talk and interaction, as those concerned search for, designate, and respond to the real or its facsimiles as a basis for getting on with life. There is no 'time out' for the task of conveying or discerning authenticity, if one seeks to be a credible member of a course of interaction and scene of everyday living."[8] Authenticity can be interactionally achieved through strategies such as privileged positioning (claiming to be an insider) and witnessing (claiming an eyewitness account). It is purposeful work that requires the skillful, craftlike giving and receiving of impression.[9]

These perspectives highlight the socially constructed, time-bound, and context-specific nature of authenticity, which, rather than an inherent descriptive property, is a social accomplishment. I argue that the social interactions within which authenticity is established, however, are embedded within power relations, organizational practices, state policies, colonial histories, and social norms. Authenticity depends on the social location of those claiming as well as those evaluating truth claims, and these pre-exist any individual interaction. Despite the fact that the "origin" of the acceptance of authenticity claims can be difficult to trace, this study of transnational service workers reveals that authenticity remains an important normative practice through which inclusion and exclusion is exercised. Accordingly, one of the central concerns of this book has been to explore transnational social and economic relations, and how these impact and are impacted by authenticity work.

This analysis of authenticity work builds on work that traces its connections to capitalist relations[10] and practices of racialized othering.[11] The management of customer perception of authenticity has been identified as "the new business imperative."[12] Indeed, everywhere around us we witness the marketing of products on the basis of their authenticity. Customers respond to the highly staged manifestation of the experience economy by demanding authenticity through customer choice of products such as the Build-a-Bear Workshop, in which customers construct their own stuffed animal, which is unique and more valuable than mass-produced versions.[13] Indeed, a vast body of work in management has emerged in the past decade on methods for ensuring authenticity in interactions between customers and workers. The seemingly liberating requirement that workers should "be themselves" at work as a way of providing authentic service can be an exercise of corporate domination and control of workers' nonwork social lives where their "authentic" selves are assumed to reside. In a case study of a call center in Australia, Peter Fleming shows how workers are encouraged to express their unique, personalized identities. However, sanctioned displays of individuality such as lifestyle choices and sexualities are encouraged, while other expressions, such as critique and negativity are pathologized. Workers can have fun and be themselves within highly controlled work processes; however, only displays of one's "real self" that lead to work efficiencies are sanctioned, and the widespread call for authenticity in management discourses raises the question of "who issues this command on the one hand, and who is asked to be 'authentic' on the other."[14] For Fleming, it is clear that organized capitalism through the corporation and its management structure issues the command for authenticity. I argue, however, that when capital crosses national borders, colonial histories and racial hierarchies become inextricably intertwined. As a result, unlike the Australian workers interviewed in Fleming's study, workers in Indian call centers are not instructed to "be themselves." Rather, workers are asked to *imagine* themselves in the eyes of their Western clients. They are asked to become these imagined ideal workers, and to be believable and authentic in their emulation of this ideal. This involves making sense of hierarchies of power as well as constructions of difference and the emerging expectations. It also involves establishing legitimacy, closeness, and familiarity in light of these expectations of difference.

This authenticity work of making sense of one's construction as "Other" has been one of the central themes explored in postcolonial studies. Critical tourism studies, for example, have historically traced the role of authenticity in the marketing of the Other for commercial gain. Brian Spooner, for example, explores the Western fascination with authentic Oriental carpets and argues that these carpets are part commodities and part symbols. They epitomize the tendency of Western societies to seek authenticity in economically dependent societies. The naming of Turkish carpets as authentic establishes the interaction between dominant and dependant, namer and named.[15] Shaun Tanaka extends this analysis to study the multifaceted actors involved in this construction of West and Other. He explores the ways in which customers, chefs, and owners engage in authentication strategies within the cultural landscape of Japanese restaurants in Toronto. This involves selecting menus, ingredients, and decor that are both distinctively Japanese and yet familiar to the Canadian cosmopolitan diner. Tanaka provides a fascinating case study of a sushi chef who conceals his excellent command of English in his interaction with customers so that he can be seen to represent an authentic Japanese subject. Tanaka notes that "by essentializing cultural production and commodifying otherness, everyday aspects of culture are stripped away while racialized ideals, images and discourses are reified. Such enduring racial stereotypes provide cosmopolitan customers a palatable form of difference that is domesticated and familiar." This "staged authenticity"[16] is achieved through authenticity work.

Customer service agents' authenticity work also serves to create the identity of the Western customer. Just like the diners of Japanese restaurants who engage with Japanese culture via sushi and simultaneously reinforce their own cosmopolitanism, Western customers know themselves as benevolent, economically powerful nationalists through their interactions with transnational service providers. Transnational service work provides the landscape for the reinscription and daily, commonplace exercise of hierarchy between national subjects.

This is not to suggest, however, that Indian workers do authenticity work simply to reify the status of the Other and maintain the economic and racialized status quo. Jessica Vaquesz and Christopher Wetzel explore how aboriginal and Mexican Americans "use claims of racial authenticity as a tactic of resistance against contemporary institutionalized racism."[17] Marginalized groups sometimes use the language of racial difference to their discursive advantage by legitimizing their authenticity and disrupting the normative hierarchies in place. By drawing attention to their high-class positions and educational levels, Indian customer service workers achieve similar aims. For example, one woman responds to the allegation that Indians need training in English language by noting, "maybe we can't speak English as them [but we are]...good in three or four languages." Authenticity work involves making sense of one's place in an imagined and experienced hierarchy. It has become an increasingly important facet of work in the context of contemporary neoliberalism, where interactions between customers and workers are privatized and receive little state or public scrutiny.

Authenticity Work in the Context of Regulatory Failure

The urgent corporate demand for worker authenticity has arisen in tandem with the widespread use of automation and work intensification in customer service work globally. Fleming notes that the contemporary organizational interest in authenticity is indicative of a void and represents an attempt to compensate for this void through a false positivism. The need for authenticity is related to the limited power, control, and dignity in workers' jobs, as a result of which workers have to be mandated to act like authentic embodied subjects.[18] This book has highlighted the complex, shifting, highly contextual and continual nature of authenticity work performed by Indian customer service workers as an integral part of their jobs. Authenticity work on the part of Indian customer service workers is essential in the absence of effective enforcement of institutionalized and regulatory structures that organize the diverse forces of transnational capital, nationalist interests, colonial heritages, anonymous encounters, and ideologies of customer sovereignty that characterize their work. Workers need to engage continually in unpaid, invisible authenticity work because they work in a profession where they are seen as individual, self-made agents.[19] Aside from quitting, there are few avenues for recourse if workers face challenges on the job. It is hardly surprising, in this context, that the BPO industry in India faces a staggering 55 percent attrition rate.[20]

Despite their widely assumed "middle-class" privileged status, relative high pay, and highly sought-after jobs, workers report a shocking range of employer violations of their terms of employment. Although several worker advocacy organizations have emerged since 2000—such as the BPO Union, UNITES Professionals, and Union Network International—none of the workers interviewed had contacted or pursued their complaints. Indeed, workers report a culture of organizational impunity. Several note that they are paid less than they were promised, and that payment errors are impossible to correct: "INR 10,000 is missing from [my] yearly package. I never went to the HR. They have a lot of excuses. It's better not to go"; "My three months incentives are still pending.... After three months of nagging the HR you'll get your incentives"; "Sometimes like AP [additional productivity]... they forget to add that"; "Sometimes the cab didn't come and my TL [team leader] used to call me... 'Where are you still?' Then I used to say, like, 'Ma'am, the cab hasn't turned up.' 'You come by yourself, and we'll adjust.' Then I used to go by rick [rickshaw]. I used to pay INR 180... but nothing about settlement."

Other workers were dismissed without notice or settlement and fired for absences due to illness. This is in clear violation of the Industrial Disputes Act, which requires that an employer provide a thirty-day notice to an employee who has to be discharged.[21] Bureaucratic hurdles, however, make it difficult to take any action against employers, as explained by a recent recruit: "The company was actually growing.... On the 8th [we were told] there would be no office from today.... It was legally, officially announced that on the 9th of January the company is shutting down. The worst part was they didn't place us anywhere.... It was a top management decision.... It was a problem for me. I didn't get my confirmation on paper... I had completed six months but I never got my confirmation on paper ... I will not get [the settlement]." Another worker reported the organizational use of "on-the-job-training" (OJT) as a cost-cutting strategy because although trainees are required to take calls during this period, they do not receive incentives. She was repeatedly told that she required more training and worked for over five months without any incentives, receiving only two-thirds of the salary of others engaged in the same work. Out of her batch, which consisted of twenty-seven new recruits, only two had been successful in obtaining the necessary scores to leave OJT.

Despite being outraged by these experiences, workers responded by changing jobs or planning future job shifts rather than confronting employers directly or launching complaints. This is not surprising given the organizational intimidation tactics in place: "[The HR manager] started scolding me, scaring me that ... if you are forcing for your salary, we will complain you then I will take you to court.... I'll take you to the police. Don't call me here again.... So I said fine, if I've wasted one month of time nothing will happen. I'll search in another job." Workers seeking any accommodation are treated like truant youth: "My grandmom was very sick.... They didn't allow me to go ... I just left and I went. So they didn't pay me.... They say give us the number of the hospital.... You're just lying, just bluffing, and we need to talk to the doctor."

Many workers reported an intensification of these practices since the recession of 2009.[22] One trainer noted that her organization had shrunk from eight hundred to five hundred employees between December 2008 and July 2009. This downsizing occurred by firing people for "errors" that had resulted in warnings in the past—such as hanging up on a caller or taking an unplanned leave. Team leaders could unilaterally and without explanation declare that an agent had committed a "fatal error" on the job, which results in immediate termination. One worker said that he was asked to leave his job for being rude to a customer. The customer had hung up after learning that he could not receive an increase in his credit limit. The dismissed worker explains: "It was not I was rude. I was just setting back myself. The customer told me to do this. I told him, see this is the reason I cannot. Then he told me to do the other thing. I said this is the reason I cannot. [The team leader] said, 'You were rude. You did not want to help the customer.'"

Even those who left jobs, however, were extremely vulnerable. Workers reported the need for a "release letter" from their employer if they wished to seek other employment. The man quoted above who had been asked to leave for alleged rudeness had been waiting for three months for this letter and had made many futile trips to the company to ask for it. Each time, he was informed that the letter was not ready because signatures from managers working in different shifts were required. Many workers reported the existence of a "blacklisting" process, which they understood as a database of unruly workers shared among call centers that could permanently sever their employment opportunities. One worker depicts the choice between leaving voluntarily or being fired: "Either you drink poison or get yourself shot." The fear of being blacklisted forced many workers to find polite and muted ways of requesting release letters or pay owed. It significantly hindered workers' ability to demand the rights entrenched in local labor law.[23]

Despite the fact that workers have full-time jobs that pay higher wages in comparison to local norms, they often face dehumanizing conditions and have little recourse when they experience employer violations of their work contract. Although some organizing efforts are underway, there are significant challenges to organizing call center workers in India, including their identities as middle-class professionals tasked with the role of protecting India's prominence as an ideal location for offshore work and the lack of better labor market alternatives. As a result, unionization efforts in the call center sector in India have avoided confrontational labor agitation and instead taken the form of employer-union partnerships that combine advocacy efforts with training and services for members.[24]

The lack of enforcement of Indian labor laws and limited opportunities for collective organizing in conjunction with employer supremacy is the framework within which transnational customer service workers in India perform their jobs. Workers are simultaneously heralded as the epitome of India's progressive, forward-looking, professional class and demeaned as recipients of privilege sought by multitudes willing to take their place. Based on their survey of the BPO sector, Phil Taylor and Peter Bain note that almost all companies have policies in place for dealing with employee grievances. The existence of these policies conveys the impression that workers' concerns are adequately addressed in-house, requiring little state intervention.[25] In line with this, the Indian government has responded to the recession of 2009 by exempting the BPO sector from local labor protection law until 2011.[26] Workers' experiences suggest the urgent need for protective policy given that the voluntary compliance of labor laws is far from the norm in most organizations.

Sameness and Difference in the Global Neoliberal Economy

This regulatory failure intensifies the need for the authenticity work of transnational service workers. Their work requires them to emulate and connect, while at the same time maintaining their position as deficient and disposable. Transnational service work is one arena where meanings of the West and India are negotiated. Joel Kahn poses the provocative question: "What does it mean to say that cultural difference has become global?" He argues that imperialist discourses are accompanied by discourses of cultural difference, and, as a result, "culture is sometimes seen as immutable, sometimes as infinitely manipulable, differences are sometimes taken to be insuperable and at other times translatable."[27] It is on this slippery terrain that Indian customer service workers establish their legitimacy as authentic, ideal workers who are just like their customers in the West and able to understand and serve their needs, and yet different enough to not pose a challenge to their economic and cultural superiority. As this book has shown, transnational service work involves a continual negotiation of customer expectations, work practices, and media constructions that arise from the dual, sometimes contradictory requirement that they be ideal transnational service workers—phone clones—who are the same and yet different from their customers in the West.

NOTES

Introduction

1. Alok Aggarwal, William Aspray, Orna Berry, Stephanie Ann Lenway, and Valerie Taylor, "Offshoring: The Big Picture," in *Globalization and Offshoring of Software: A Report of the ACM Job Migration Task Force,* ed. William Aspray, Frank Mayadas, and Moshe Y. Vardi, 10 (Association for Computing Machinery, 2006), http://www.acm.org/globalizationreport/chapter1.pdf (accessed April 21 2007).

2. John Burgess and Julia Connell, "Developments in the Call Center Sector," in *Developments in the Call Center Industry: Analysis, Changes and Challenges,* ed. John Burgess and Julia Connell, 1–17 (London: Routledge, 2006).

3. National Association of Software and Service Companies (NASSCOM), *Strategic Review 2011* (New Delhi, India: NASSCOM, 2011), http://www.nasscom.in/upload/Publications/Research/140211/Executive_Summary.pdf (accessed August 29th 2011).

4. NASSCOM, *NASSCOM-Everest India BPO Study: Roadmap 2012—Capitalizing on the Expanding BPO Landscape* (New Delhi, India: NASSCOM, 2008), 1.

5. Jayan Jose Thomas, "An Uneasy Coexistence: The New and the Old in Indian Industry and Services," in *A New India? Critical Reflections in the Long Twentieth Century,* ed. Anthony P. D'Costa, 71–98 (London: Anthem Press, 2010).

6. *Time,* June 26, 2006, cover image, http://www.time.com/time/covers/0,16641,20060626,00.html (accessed August 29, 2011).

7. Reena Patel, *Working the Night Shift: Women in India's Call Center Industry* (Palo Alto, CA: Stanford University Press, 2010), 37. Patel notes that the wedding attire in this image signifies the underlying theme of marriage—between East and West; tradition and Western development.

8. Anshuman Prasad and Pushkala Prasad, "Otherness at Large: Identity and Difference in the New Globalized Organizational Landscape," in *Gender, Identity and the Culture of Organizations,* ed. I. Aaltio and A. J. Mills, 57–71, 62 (London: Routledge, 2002).

9. Theo Van Leeuwen, "What Is Authenticity," *Discourse Studies* 3, no. 4 (2001): 393.

10. Ibid., 393.

11. Jennie Germann Molz, "Eating Difference: The Cosmopolitan Mobilities of Culinary Tourism," *Space and Culture* 10, no. 1 (2007): 86.

12. James H. Gilmore and B. Joseph Pine II, *Authenticity: What Consumers Really Want* (Boston: Harvard Business School Press, 2007), 3; B. Joseph Pine and James H. Gilmore, *The Experience Economy* (Boston: Harvard Business School Press, 1999). Gilmore and Pine argue that the growth of experience-based commerce has left customers with a desire for less staged and more authentic experiences. As a result, organizations have to manage customer perceptions of authenticity to gain competitive advantage.

13. Selma K. Sonntag, "Linguistic Globalization and the Call Center Industry: Imperialism, Hegemony or Cosmopolitanism?" *Language Policy* 8, no. 1 (2009): 17.

14. Carol Upadhya, "Management of Culture and Management through Culture in the Indian Software Outsourcing Industry," in *An Outpost of the Global Economy: Work and Workers in India's Information Technology Industry,* ed. C. Upadhya and A. R. Vasavi, 101–35, 103 (New Delhi, India: Routledge, 2008).

15. Sara Ahmed, *Strange Encounters: Embodied Others in Post-Coloniality* (London: Routledge, 2000), 3, 8 (see Chapter 2, n. 4).

16. Ibid., see Chapter 3, note 20.

17. Avlar Brah, "Difference, Diversity, Differentiation," in *Feminism and "Race,"* ed. Kum-Kum Bhavnani, 456–78 (Oxford: Oxford University Press, 2001).

18. A. Aneesh, *Virtual Migration: The Programming of Globalization* (Durham, NC: Duke University Press, 2006), 93.

19. Philomena Essed and David Theo Goldberg, "Cloning Cultures: The Social Injustices of Sameness," *Ethnic and Racial Studies* 25, no. 6 (2002): 1066–82.

20. Ibid., 1070.

21. Kamal Nath, *India's Century: The Age of Entrepreneurship in the World's Biggest Democracy* (New York: McGraw-Hill Books, 2008), 10; NASSCOM, *NASSCOM-Everest India BPO Study: Roadmap 2012,* 1. Figures on the numbers of employees working in call centers are difficult to obtain because statistics are often reported for the IT/ITES sector as a whole. The number of BPO jobs include those working in back-office (email) as well as voice processes.

22. Huck Gutman, "Outsourcing in the Developed and Developing World. Part Two: The Age of India Cometh," *Statesman,* March 24, 2004, http://www.commondreams.org/views04/0325-08.htm (accessed September 1, 2005).

23. BBC News, "Call Centers 'Bad for India,'" November 11, 2003, http://news.bbc.co.uk/2/hi/south_asia/3292619.stm (accessed September 1, 2005).

24. Others who have interviewed workers have reached a similar conclusion; see, e.g., Shehzad Nadeem, *Dead Ringers: How Outsourcing Is Changing the Way Indians Understand Themselves* (Princeton, NJ: Princeton University Press, 2011); Patel, *Working the Night Shift* (see n. 7 above).

25. This is in line with theorists such as Carla Freeman, *High Tech and High Heels in the Global Economy: Women, Work, and Pink-Collar Identities in the Caribbean* (Durham, NC: Duke University Press, 2000); Marek Korczynski and Cameron Lynne Macdonald, "Critical Perspectives on Service Work: An Introduction," in *Service Work: Critical Perspectives,* ed. Marek Korczynski and Cameron Lynne Macdonald, 1–10 (New York: Routledge, 2009); Diane van den Broek, "Globalising Call Center Capital: Gender, Culture and Work Identity," *Labor & Industry* 14, no. 3 (2004): 59–75.

26. Harriet Bradley, Mark Erickson, Carol Stephenson, and Steve Williams, *Myths at Work* (Cambridge: Polity Press, 2000), 9; Susanne Bergeron, "Political Economy Discourses of Globalization and Feminist Politics," *Signs* 26, no. 4 (2001): 983–1006; Saskia Sassen, "Cracked Casings: Notes Towards an Analytics for Studying Transnational Processes," in *New Transnational Social Spaces: International Migration and Transnational Companies in the Early Twenty-First Century,* ed. Ludger Pries, 187–207 (London: Routledge, 2001).

27. Carla Freeman, "Is Local: Global as Feminine: Masculine? Rethinking the Gender of Globalization," *Signs* 26, no. 4 (2001): 1008–1009. Emphasis added.

28. Ahmed, *Strange Encounters,* 22 (italics removed).

29. Anne Witz, Chris Warhurst, and Dennis Nickson, "The Labor of Aesthetics and the Aesthetics of Organization," *Organization* 10, no. 1 (2003): 33–54. In developing the term "aesthetic labor," Witz and her colleagues note that organizations not only purchase employees' soft skills or emotional labor but workers also form part of the organizations' hardware by looking a particular way. This is the physical capital of employees, which is transformed, through training, into the economic capital of organizations.

30. Six sigma is a quality measurement tool originally developed by Motorola in 1986. It involves following a set of strategies to minimize the error rate in the manufacturing process.

31. The term *emotion work* has been used to describe the relational work that people do as part of their paid jobs. Chapter 5 focuses on Indian call center workers' emotion work.

32. David Theo Goldberg, *The Threat of Race: Reflections on Racial Neoliberalism* (Malden, MA: Wiley-Blackwell, 2009). Goldberg (p. 336) notes that the hallmark of neoliberal racism is the transformation of systemic racism into forms of private expression. He provides the example of the Minutemen, a self-declared border patrol group who post slogans such as "This is America, get off my property." Rather than an expression of racist discrimination in need of state sanction, the group is seen to be exercising its right to freedom of expression. In a similar way, customers in the West exercise their right to condemn outsourcing via racist anger with no social or legal repercussions.

33. Barbara Adam, "The Gendered Time Politics of Globalization: Of Shadowlands and Elusive Justice," *Feminist Review* 70 (2002): 3–29, 21, http://www.feminist-review.com (accessed September 1, 2003). As Adam notes, capital is assumed to have a constantly ticking clock. This is the "commodification of time," in which each part of the production process is conceptualized in terms of time—such as labor time, the time for which a machine lasts, the time for which materials have to be stored, and so forth (ibid., 17). The combined export of Western clock time and commodified time is the colonization *with* time (ibid., 21).

1. Transnational Customer Service

1. The phrase "great employment sponge" was coined by Bob Russell, "Skill and Info-Service Work in Australian Call Centers," in *Developments in the Call Center Industry: Analysis, Changes and Challenges,* ed. John Burgess and Julia Connell, 92–116 (London: Routledge, 2006), to refer to the rapid rate at which the service economy has absorbed labor over the past thirty years. Similar observations have been made by Winifred R. Poster, "Saying 'Good Morning' in the Night: The Reversal of Work Time in Global ICT Service Work," in *Research in the Sociology of Work* 17 (2007): 63, who has analyzed International Labor Organization (ILO) data and summarizes that "most new jobs within the formal sector around the world are in services. . . . [T]hese jobs involve doing something for people rather than making things." See also Jeff Hearn, "Feeling Out of Place? Towards the Transnationalization of Emotions," in *The Emotional Organization: Passions and Power,* ed. Stephen Fineman, 184–201 (Malden, MA: Blackwell, 2008); Debra Howcroft and Helen Richardson, "Gender Matters in the Global Outsourcing of Service Work," *New Technology, Work and Employment* 23, nos. 1–2 (2008): 44–60.

2. Benjamin R. Barber, *Jihad vs. McWorld* (New York: Random House, 1995), 75, http://www.theatlantic.com/magazine/archive/1992/03/jihad-vs-mcworld/3882/ (accessed August 29, 2011).

3. Ronnie J. Steinberg and Deborah M. Figart, "Emotional Labor Since: The Managed Heart, *The Annals of the American Academy of Political and Social Science* 561, no. 1 (1999): 8–26. Theorists also note that service work is gendered in the context of "women's allegedly greater facility with emotions—the feminine capacity to console and comfort, flatter, cajole, persuade and seduce" (Hannah Frith and Celia Kitzinger, "'Emotion Work' as a Participant Resource: A Feminist Analysis of Young Women's Talk-in-Interaction," *Sociology* 32, no. 2 (1998): 299–320). Along the same lines, Elaine J. Hall, "Smiling, Deferring, and Flirting: Doing Gender by Giving 'Good Service,'" *Work and Occupations* 20, no. 4 (1993): 452–71, argues that service work is often considered an extension of women's roles in the home. Restaurants, for example, construct and legitimate a gendered image of the server as deferential servant.

4. Linda McDowell provides a review of this literature in *Working Bodies: Interactive Service Employment and Workplace Identities* (Sussex: Blackwell Publishing, 2009).

5. Winifred R. Poster and George Wilson, "Introduction: Race, Class, and Gender in Transnational Labor Inequality," *American Behavioral Scientist* 52, no. 3 (2008): 295–306, 301.

6. Rafiq Dossani and Martin Kenney, "The Next Wave of Globalization: Relocating Service Provision to India," *World Development* 35, no. 5 (2007): 772–91, trace the historical trajectory of services offshoring, noting that it was an outcome of the trend toward subcontracting that firms adopted to take advantage of lower labor costs in smaller towns in the United States in the 1960s. With the development of effective telecommunications technology, this work could be moved farther away geographically.

7. Employment in call centers in India has grown from a hundred thousand workers in 2001 to seven hundred thousand in 2008 (NASSCOM, *NASSCOM-Everest India BPO Study: Roadmap 201—Capitalizing on the Expanding BPO Landscape* [New Delhi, India: NASSCOM, 2008]). This is part of the overall growth in the IT and IT-enabled services (ITES) sector, which now employs over two million people in India (NASSCOM, *Impact of IT-BPO Industry in India: A Decade in Review* (New Delhi, India: NASSCOM, 2010), http://www.nasscom.in/upload/68924/Impact_Study_2010_Exec_Summary.pdf (accessed August 29, 2011). Also see Rosemary Batt, David Holman, and Ursula Holtgrewe, "The Globalization of Service Work: Comparative Institutional Perspectives on Call Centers: Introduction to a Special Issue of ILRR," *Industrial and Labor Relations Review* 62, no. 4 (2009): 453–88; Pawan Budhwar, Neeru Malhotra, and Virender Singh, "Work Processes and Emerging Problems in Indian Call Centers," in *The Next Available Operator: Managing Human Resources in Indian Business Process Outsourcing Industry,* ed. Mohan Thite and Bob Russell, 59–82 (New Delhi, India: Response Books, 2009).

8. Arjun Appadurai addresses the relationship between histories and geographies. He notes that geographies are often assumed to be fixed, physical spaces around which histories occur. He proposes, instead, that histories give rise to geographies since cities and nations are all recent, artificial products of human intervention. Arjun Appadurai, "The New and the Now: Globalization and the Politics of the Déjà Vu" (lecture, Munk School of Global Affairs, University of Toronto on October 22, 2010).

9. As Amita Gupta, "Tracing Global-Local Transitions within Early Childhood Curriculum and Practices in India," *Research in Comparative and International Education* 3, no. 3 (2008): 266–80, shows, "educational institutions established under the colonial rule reflected attempts to reproduce all aspects of education in European institutions, including curriculum, pedagogy, hierarchal organization, architecture and even codes of conduct for students" (274).

10. Batt et al., "Globalization of Service Work," 464–65.

11. Kunal Sen, "New Interpretations of India's Economic Growth in the Twentieth Century," in *A New India? Critical Reflections in the Long Twentieth Century,* ed. Anthony P. D'Costa,

23–42 (London: Anthem Press, 2010), argues that the reasons for India's economic growth predate 1991 reforms.

12. Rob Jenkins, "The Politics of India's Special Economic Zones," in *Understanding India's New Political Economy: A Great Transformation?,* ed. Sanjay Ruparelia, Sanjay Reddy, John Harriss, and Stuart Corbridge (Oxon, UK: Routledge, 2011), 1–16. Jenkins provides a history of the establishment of Special Economic Zones (SEZs) and the passage of the Special Economic Zones Act in 2005 (7). See also A. R. Vasavi, "'Serviced from India': The Making of India's Global Youth Workforce," in *In an Outpost of the Global Economy: Work and Workers in India's Information Technology Industry,* ed. Carol Upadhya and A. R. Vasavi, 211–34 (New Delhi, India: Routledge, 2008).

13. Swasti Mitter, Grace Fernandez, and Shaiby Varghese, "On the Threshold of Informalization: Women Call Centre Workers in India," in *Chains of Fortune: Linking Women Producers and Workers with Global Markets,* ed. Marilyn Carr, 165–84 (London: Commonwealth Secretariate, 2004). Mitter and colleagues note there is little planning to ensure that frontline workers "do not bear the brunt of sudden adjustments if foreign companies pull out and some jobs disappear" (168).

14. Sareeta Amrute, "Living and Praying the Code: The Flexibility and Discipline of Indian Information Technology Workers (ITers) in a Global Economy," *Anthropological Quarterly* 83, no. 3 (2010): 519–50, traces the concurrent emergence of economic modernization and religious conservatism in the 1990s, 527.

15. Dossani and Kenney, "The Next Wave," *World Development* 35, no. 5 (2007): 772–91; Bob Russell, "Call Centers: A Decade of Research," *International Journal of Management Reviews* 10, no. 3 (2008): 195–219.

16. Saskia Sassen, "Cracked Casings: Notes toward an Analytics for Studying Transnational Processes," in *New Transnational Social Spaces: International Migration and Transnational Companies in the Early Twenty-First Century,* ed. Ludger Pries, 187–207 (London: Routledge, 2001). Sassen uses the term "strategic agents" to refer to elite global actors who manage and coordinate the global economy. Also see Navdeep Suri, "Offshore Outsourcing of Services as a Catalyst of Economic Development: The Case of India," in *Global Capitalism Unbound: Winners and Losers from Offshore Outsourcing,* ed. Eva Paus, 163–79 (Basingstoke, England: Palgrave Macmillan, 2007).

17. A. Aneesh, *Virtual Migration: The Programming of Globalization* (Durham, NC: Duke University Press, 2006), terms this movement of work without workers "virtual migration."

18. Marek Korczynski, *Human Resource Management in Service Work* (Basingstoke, England: Palgrave Macmillan, 2002).

19. The emotion work of Indian customer service agents will be discussed in Chapter 5.

20. Dossani and Kenney, "The Next Wave," 195; Russell, "Call Centers," 8–12.

21. Anna Greenspan, *India and the IT Revolution: Networks of Global Culture* (Basingstoke, England: Palgrave Macmillan, 2004), 93.

22. Michael Palm, "Outsourcing, Self-Service and the Telemobility of Work, *Anthropology of Work Review* 27, no. 2 (2006): 1–9; Francesco Stolfi and Gerald J. Sussman, "Telecommunications and Transnationalism: The Polarization of Social Space," *The Information Society* 17 (2001): 49–62.

23. Paul Davies, *What's This India Business? Offshoring, Outsourcing, and the Global Services Revolution* (New York: Nicholas Braeley International, 2004), 46.

24. Edward Alden, "Cost Differentials and Labor Flexibility Mean Opportunity for Outsourcing," *The Financial Times and Yale Global Online,* January 28, 2004, http://yaleglobal.yale.edu/content/cost-differentials-and-labour-flexibility-mean-opportunity-outsourcing (accessed August 2011).

25. Russell, "Call Centers," *International Journal of Management Reviews* 10, no. 3 (2008): 199, notes that "call center work is the information economy's equivalent of semi-skilled labor,

meaning that employment entails greater skill than the blue-collar operator positions of the factory era, but cannot be meaningfully considered knowledge work."

26. Thite and Russell, eds., *The Next Available Operator: Managing Human Resources in Indian Business Process Outsourcing Industry* (New Delhi, India: Response Books, 2009), 255.

27. Poster, "Saying 'Good Morning,'" *Research in the Sociology of Work* 17 (2007): 65.

28. Mathangi Krishnamurthy, "Resources and Rebels: A Study of Identity Management in Indian Call Centers," *Anthropology of Work Review* 25, nos. 3–4 (2004): 9–18; Leela Fernandes, *India's New Middle Class: Democratic Politics in an Era of Economic Reform* (Minneapolis: University of Minnesota Press, 2006).

29. Diane Reay, "Rethinking Social Class: Qualitative Perspectives on Class and Gender," *Sociology* 32, no. 2 (1998): 259–75, 266.

30. Aneesh, *Virtual Migration* (Durham, NC: Duke University Press, 2006), 65.

31. Winifred R. Poster, "Who's on the Line? Indian Call Center Agents Pose as Americans for U.S.-Outsourced Firms," *Industrial Relations* 46, no. 2 (2007): 271–304, terms the organizational requirement that workers adopt different identities as part of their jobs as "national identity management" (271).

32. Winifred R. Poster and George Wilson, "Introduction: Race, Class, and Gender in Transnational Labor Inequality," *American Behavioral Scientist* 52, no. 3 (2008): 295–306.

33. Edna Bonacich, Sabrina Alimahomed, and Jake B. Wilson, "The Racialization of Global Labor," *American Behavioral Scientist* 52, no. 3 (2008): 342–55, provide historical examples of links between globalization and racialization.

34. Jake Skeers, "Study Documents Exploitation in Indian Call Centres," International Committee of the Fourth International (ICFI), *World Socialist Web Site* (November 23, 2005), 1, http://www.wsws.org/articles/2005/nov2005/indi-23n.shtml (accessed September 1, 2006).

35. Kathi Weeks, "Life Within and Against Work: Affective Labor, Feminist Critique, and Post-Fordist Politics," *Ephemera: Theory & Politics in Organization* 7, no. 1 (2007): 233–49, 238, http://www.ephemeraweb.org/journal/index.htm (accessed April 21, 2009); see also Lisa Adkins and Eeva Jokinen, "Introduction: Gender, Living and Labor in the Fourth Shift," *NORA—Nordic Journal of Feminist and Gender Research* 16, no. 3 (2008): 138–49.

36. Diane van den Broek, "Globalising Call Center Capital: Gender, Culture and Identity," *Labor & Industry* 14, no. 3 (2004): 59–75, notes that "workers literally embody the service they provide. So rather than producing tangible products like cars or clothing, interactive service workers and call center workers particularly, trade in aesthetics and emotions—that is, workers sell attitude, personality and voice" (60).

37. Reena Patel, "Working the Night Shift: Gender and the Global Economy," *ACME: An International E-Journal for Critical Geographies* 5, no. 1 (2006): 9–27, 21, http://www.acme-journal.org/index.html (accessed April 21, 2009).

38. Sanjukta Mukherjee, "Producing the IT Miracle: The Neoliberalizing States and Changing Gender and Class Regimes in India" (doctoral dissertation, Syracuse University, 2008). Available from ProQuest Dissertations and Theses database. Mukherjee's study of IT professionals similarly reveals that professional women depend on parents, in-laws, and domestic help.

39. Saskia Sassen, "Two Stops in Today's New Global Geographies: Shaping Novel Labor Supplies and Employment Regimes," *American Behavioral Scientist* 52, no. 3 (2008): 457–96, 464.

40. Marek Korczynski, *Human Resource Management in Service Work* (Basingstoke, England: Palgrave Macmillan, 2002), 2.

41. Palm, "Outsourcing, Self-Service," *Anthropology of Work Review* 27, no. 2 (2006): 6.

42. Russell, "Call Centers," *International Journal of Management Reviews* 10, no. 3 (2008): 196, argues that many researchers "have found in the call center novel and intriguing sites from which to study a host of other matters"; see also Bob Russell, *Smiling Down the Line: Info-Service Work in the Global Economy* (Toronto: University of Toronto Press, 2009).

43. Margaret Abraham, "Globalization and the Call Center Industry," *International Sociology* 23, no. 2 (2008): 197–210, 198; see also Ursula Huws, "Working at the Interface: Call-Centre Labour in a Global Economy," *Work Organisation, Labour & Globalisation* 3, no. 1 (2009): 1–8, http://analytica.metapress.com/content/c7212881 0j7357u3/fulltext.pdf (accessed August 29, 2011).

44. For findings from the early stages of data collection, see Kiran Mirchandani, "Gender Eclipsed? Racial Hierarchies in Transnational Call Centres," *Social Justice* 32, no. 4 (2006): 105–19, revised and reprinted in Kiran Mirchandani, "Gendered Hierarchies in Transnational Call Centres," in *Work and Life in the Global Economy,* ed. Debra Howcroft and Helen Richardson, 78–98 (Hampshire, UK: Palgrave Macmillan, 2004); Kiran Mirchandani, "Practices of Global Capital: Gaps, Cracks and Ironies in Transnational Call Centres in India," *Global Networks: A Journal of Transnational Affairs* 4, no. 4 (2004): 355–74, reprinted in Mirchandani, "Transnationalism in Indian Call Centres," in *The Next Available Operator,* ed. Mohan Thite and Bob Russell, 83–114 (New Delhi, India: Sage, 2009); also reprinted in Mirchandani, "Practices of Global Capital: Gaps, Cracks and Ironies in Transnational Call Centres," in *South Asian Technospaces,* ed. Radhika Gajjala and Venkataramana Gajjala, 225–48 (New York: Peter Lang, 2008); Kiran Mirchandani, "Enactments of Class and Nationality in Transnational Call Centres," in *The Emotional Organization: Passions and Power,* ed. Stephen Fineman, 88–101 (Oxford: Blackwell, 2008); also translated into Italian, "Le Emozioni Nell' Organizzazone" (Milano: Rafello Cortina Editore, 2009); Kiran Mirchandani, "Webs of Resistance in Transnational Call Centers: Strategic Agents, Service Providers and Customers," in *Identity Politics at Work: Resisting Gender, Gendering Resistance,* ed. Robyn Thomas, Albert J. Mills, and Jean Helms Mills, 179–95 (London: Routledge, 2004); Kiran Mirchandani and Srabani Maitra, "Learning Imperialism through Transnational Call Centres," in *Educating the Global Workforce: Knowledge Work, Knowledge Workers,* ed. Tara Fenwick, 154–64 (London: Routledge, 2007); Kiran Mirchandani, Srabani Maitra, and Jasjit Sangha, "Treats and Threats: Global Cultures in India's Call Centers," in *Against the Grain: Advances in Postcolonial Organization Studies,* ed. Anshuman Prasad (forthcoming).

45. National Association of Software and Service Companies-McKinsey (2005), *Extending India's Leadership of the Global IT and BPO Industries* (New Delhi: Nasscom-McKinsey). This report revealed that significant growth in the IT/ITES sector was being experienced in smaller cities such as Pune.

46. Stuart Hall, "The West and the Rest: Discourse and Power," in *Modernity: An Introduction to Modern Societies,* ed. Stuart Hall, David Held, Don Hubert, and Kenneth Thompson, 184–227 (Malden, MA: Blackwell, 1996), notes that the "rest" played a pivotal role in the formation of the idea of the "West." Rather than a geographical location, the West is an ideology through which a standard can be established and societies classified and hierarchically ranked according to this standard.

47. My methodology predates but bears many similarities to the notion of "personal narrative analysis" as described by Mary Jo Maynes, Jennifer L. Pierce, and Barbara Laslett, *Telling Stories: The Use of Personal Narratives in the Social Sciences and History* (Ithaca, NY: Cornell University Press, 2008). Focus was on understanding the agency of workers in the context of their interpretations of their social structures. I paid particular attention to workers' historical accounts of their work lives.

48. "Hinglish" is the fluid and intuitive combination of words from English and Hindi.

49. Al James and Bhaskar Vira, "'Unionising' the New Spaces of the New Economy? Alternative Labour Organizing in India's IT Enabled Services—Business Process Outsourcing Industry," *Geoforum* 41, no. 3 (2010): 364–76.

50. James Lamott, "US Proves Call Centre Match for India Over Hire Costs," *Financial Times,* August 18, 2010.

51. Bob Russell, *Smiling Down the Line: Info-Service Work in the Global Economy* (Toronto: University of Toronto Press, 2009), 12.

52. Batt et al., "Globalization of Service Work," *Industrial and Labor Relations Review* 62, no. 4 (2009): 459.

53. Other researchers, such as Reena Patel, *Working the Night Shift: Women in India's Call Center Industry* (Palo Alto, CA: Stanford University Press, 2010), and Jennifer Jarman, "Envisioning Futures in Work and Career in Large Transnational Call Centres in India," in *Trade, Labour and Transformation of Community in Asia,* ed. Michael Gillian and Bob Pokrant, 257–80 (Hampshire, UK: Palgrave Macmillan, 2009), have come to similar conclusions.

54. Drucilla K. Barker and Susan F. Feiner, "Affect, Race, and Class: An Interpretive Reading of Caring Labor," *Frontiers: A Journal of Women's Studies* 30, no. 1 (2009): 41–54, 43.

2. Language Training

1. Sara Ahmed, *Strange Encounters: Embodied Others in Post-Coloniality* (London: Routledge, 2000), 11.

2. Anne Witz, Chris Warhurst, and Dennis Nickson, "The Labor of Aesthetics and the Aesthetics of Organization," *Organization* 10, no. 1 (2003): 33–54.

3. In the context of jobs that are seen to be highly privileged, workers do not necessarily construct their attempts to speak like Americans as an imperialist practice. Rather, as Selma K. Sonntag, "Linguistic Globalization and the Call Center Industry: Imperialism, Hegemony or Cosmopolitanism?" *Language Policy* 8, no. 1 (2009): 17, has also observed, "they do not perceive themselves as imitators, or as being inauthentic." Learning to speak "correctly" is a skill to be acquired for personal success.

4. Ahmed, *Strange Encounters,* 13. Ahmed argues that the stranger "only becomes a figure through proximity." Recognizing a figure as strange or alien allows the collective formation of the boundary between the known/knowable and the unknowable/strange. In this sense, the stranger is not that which is unknown but that which is placed outside this boundary. The boundary between recognizable and strange is enacted through encounters, such as those between customer service workers in India and customers in the West.

5. Anshuman Prasad and Pushkala Prasad, "Otherness at Large: Identity and Difference in the New Globalized Organizational Landscape," in *Gender, Identity and the Culture of Organizations,* ed. I. Aaltio and A. J. Mills (London: Routledge, 2002), 57–71, 65.

6. Claire Cowie, The "Accents of Outsourcing: The Meanings of 'Neutral' in the Indian Call Center Industry," *World Englishes* 26, no. 3 (2007): 316–30.

7. Witz et al., "Labor of Aesthetics," *Organization* 10, no. 1 (2003): 41 (see also Introduction, n. 29).

8. As Sharon C. Bolton, "Conceptual Confusions: Emotion Work as Skilled Work," in *The Skills That Matter: Critical Perspectives on Work and Organisations,* ed. Chris Warhurst, Irena Grugulis, and Ewart Keep (Basingstoke, England: Palgrave Macmillan, 2004), 19–37, observes, "the frontline service worker is frequently the only contact a customer has with an organization making the quality of interaction a major criterion on which the organization is judged" (27).

9. Binoo K. John, *Entry from Backside Only: Hazaar Fundas* [one thousand techniques] *of Indian-English* (New Delhi, India: Penguin Books, 2007); see also Véronique Bénéï, "Of Languages, Passions and Interests: Education, Regionalism and Globalization in Maharashtra," in *Globalizing India: Perspectives from Below,* ed. Jackie Assayag and Chris J. Fuller (London: Anthem Press, 2005), 141–62.

10. John, *Entry from Backside Only,* 59, 66.

11. Shehzad Nadeem, "Macaulay's (Cyber) Children: The Cultural Politics of Outsourcing in India," *Cultural Sociology* 3 (2009): 102–22, 112.

12. Based on their participant observation of training sessions in Kolkata call centers, Diya Das, Ravi Dharwadkar, and Pamela Brandes, "The Importance of Being 'Indian': Identity

Centrality and Work Outcomes in an Off-shored Call Center in India," *Human Relations* 61, no. 11 (2008): 1499–1530, note the frequent use of mockery to draw attention to Indianisms. Trainers use humorous examples designed to inculcate shame of stereotypical, so-called Indian ways of speaking. These protocols, in conjunction with "marks" based on performance measures such as speaking slowly, using pronunciations deemed neutral, and avoiding Hindi fillers routinely awarded to trainees serve to stratify trainees and weed out particular workers.

13. Monica Heller, "Language, Skill and Authenticity in the Globalized New Economy," *Noves SL. Revista de Sociolingüística* 2 (2005), http://www6.gencat.cat/llengcat/noves/hm05hivern/docs/heller.pdf (accessed April 21, 2006). Heller provides a fascinating analysis of how language is converted into a work-related competence through an analysis of the call center industry in New Brunswick, Canada, which is marketed as bilingual (English and French) on the basis of an Acadian workforce. Heller notes that implicit connections between ethnicity and language proficiency are implicitly assumed.

14. Arjun Raina, *Speak Right for a Call Center Job! A Complete Training Guide for International Telephonic Interface* (New Delhi, India: Penguin Books, 2004); Madhukar Yadav, *Winning @ Call Centre: Confessions of a Calling Agent* (New Delhi, India: Wisdom Tree, 2007); Namrata Palta, *Preparing for Call Center Interviews* (New Delhi, India: Lotus Press, 2007).

15. John, *Entry from Backside Only,* 167.

16. The analysis in this section is based on the two sets of training manuals provided by respondents. One set of documents contains no copyright or author information. Another document mentions a specific global human resource organization as the publisher. The two spiral-bound documents contain the name of the organization and the word "confidential" at the bottom of each page.

17. John M. Swales, "English as 'Tyrannosaurus Rex,'" *World Englishes* 16, no. 3 (1997): 373–82. Swales discussion of "language trafficking" refers to the multimillion-dollar industry surrounding the promotion and teaching of the English language around the world (377).

18. Sonntag, "Linguistic Globalization," 21.

19. Laurie Cohen and Amal El-Sawad, "Accounting for 'Us' and 'Them': Indian and UK Customer Service Workers' Reflections on Offshoring," *Economic and Political Weekly* 42, no. 21 (2007): 1951–57, 1957, http://hum.sagepub.com/content/60/8/1235.short (accessed August 23, 2011).

20. Bénéï, "Languages, Passions and Interests," 141–62, traces this link between the use of English and the ruling classes in colonial India: That "the English language enjoys a dominant position in the financial, economic and technological domains in India today is by no means a recent phenomenon. Rather, it goes back to colonial times and the construction of the British Empire, with which English was closely associated from the early nineteenth century. English then was not only the language of the British, as we all know, but also that of the British *Empire*... consequently, acquisition of the language as also a gateway to local administrative positions for some sections of the indigenous population"(146).

21. John, *Entry from Backside Only,* 106, 108, 114. English is ironically both the language of progress and the language of colonial oppression. This dual construction complicates the relationship between language and class, and provokes diverse and unexpected responses. Examples include Bénéï's "Languages, Passions and Interests," fieldwork which reveals that middle-class Maharashtrans prefer Marathi medium schools over English medium schools despite the widespread acknowledgment of the utility of English in the labor market. Srivastava, quoted in John, *Entry from Backside Only,* 109, recounts that a Hindi-speaking North Indian family may speak to one another in public in English, while a family with transnational linkages and a longer and more secure history of English-language usage within the family may speak in the local language in public. These examples reveal the complex and shifting normative hierarchies between English and regional languages in contemporary India that exist alongside the historical connections between English and class privilege.

22. Mathangi Krishnamurthy, "Resources and Rebels: A Study of Identity Management in Indian Call Centers," *Anthropology of Work Review* 25, nos. 3–4 (2004): 9–18; she notes that the rapid proliferation of call centers in India is "a very particular outcome of colonial and post-colonial nationalist legacies of language prioritization" (11).

23. This quote appears in a confidential *Certificate in Customer Service: Student Guide-I,* 16.2, 16.4, training manual.

24. Carol Upadhya, "Management of Culture and Management Through Culture in the Indian Software Outsourcing Industry," in *An Outpost of the Global Economy: Work and Workers in India's Information Technology Industry,* ed. C. Upadhya and A. R. Vasavi (New Delhi, India: Routledge, 2008), 101–35.

25. Stuart Hall, "The West and the Rest: Discourse and Power," in *Modernity: An Introduction to Modern Societies,* ed. Stuart Hall, David Held, Don Hubert, and Kenneth Thompson (Malden, MA: Blackwell, 1996), 184–227, 196.

3. Hate Nationalism

1. John Downey and Natalie Fenton, "Global Capital, Local Resistance? Trade Unions, National Newspapers and the Symbolic Contestation of 'Offshoring' in the UK," *Current Sociology* 55, no. 5 (2007): 651–73, note that "global corporations are profit led and seek out places of production that offer greater efficiency and competitiveness. Place loyalty or obligations to local workforces are, on the whole, ignored" (654). At the same time, given the concentration of capital in the West, trade agreements and capital flows are affected by the expressed national interests of countries such as the United States or United Kingdom.

2. Mark Landler, "Hi, I'm in Bangalore (but I Can't Say So)," *New York Times,* March 21, 2001, http://www.nytimes.com/2001/03/21/technology/21CALL.html?scp = 1&sq = %22I'm%20 in%20Bangalore%22&st = cse. The quote appears on 1 of the Technology section (accessed September 1, 2001).

3. Winifred R. Poster, "Who's on the Line? Indian Call Center Agents Pose as Americans for U.S.-Outsourced Firms," *Industrial Relations* 46, no. 2 (2007): 271–304. Poster argues that the protocol whereby workers in Indian call centers are required to mask their geographical location is part of the new managerial strategy called "national identity management" whereby workers are required to construct appropriate self-identities as part of their jobs. Ibid., 272.

4. Greg Sitt, Diverted to Delhi (New York: Filmmakers Library, 2007), *quoted in* Diya Das, Ravi Dharwadkar, and Pamela Brandes, "The Importance of Being 'Indian': Identity Centrality and Work Outcomes in an Off-shored Call Center in India," *Human Relations* 61, no. 11 (2008): 1499–1530, 1508.

5. Arjun Appadurai, *Modernity at Large: Cultural Dimensions of Globalization* (Minneapolis: University of Minnesota Press, 1996), 41. Appadurai uses the term "production fetishism" to refer to the ways in which the ownership of a company in a particular country or area does not necessarily lead to wealth creation for that same country. Also Selma K. Sonntag, "Linguistic Globalization and the Call Center Industry: Imperialism, Hegemony or Cosmopolitanism?" *Language Policy* 8, no. 1 (2009): 5–25, notes, global "companies are absolved of responsibility, benefitting their self portrayal as nation-less, agency-less, global entities" (14). Responsibility for offshoring is seen to lie with individual Indians rather than corporate policies.

6. Landler, "Hi, I'm in Bangalore," 1.

7. Phil Taylor, Premilla D'Cruz, Ernesto Noronha, and Dora Scholarios, "Domestic Labour: The Experience of Work in India's Other Call Centre Industry," in *Work and Life in the Global Economy: A Gendered Analysis of Service Work,* ed. Debra Howcroft and Helen Richardson (New York: Palgrave Macmillan, 2010), 99–123. Taylor notes that many decisions that fundamentally affect call centers in India are made in corporate boardrooms in the West.

8. This is similar to a process described in Sara Ahmed, *Strange Encounters* (New York: Routledge, 2000), and in Sara Ahmed, *The Cultural Politics of Emotion* (New York: Routledge,

2004). Ahmed notes that identities are constituted via encounters. She describes the process of recognizing strangers, establishing boundaries through defining strangers as dangerous, and exercising hate.

9. Interestingly, responses to outsourcing to India are more muted in Canada even though large corporations such as Bell Canada and Air Canada have service centers in India. This is likely due to Canada's dual position as originator and recipient of outsourced work (John Tennant, "Outsourcing Services: Threat or Opportunity?" *Business Times,* no. 7 (July 2004): 7, http://www.w2n2.ca/Websites/w2n2/Images/businesstimes/2004–07%20July%20JDT%20editorial.pdf (accessed September 1, 2005).

10. National Foundation for American Policy (NFAP), *NFAP Policy Brief: Anti-Outsourcing Efforts Down But Not Out* (April 2007), 1, http://www.nfap.com/pdf/0407OutsourcingBrief.pdf (accessed September 1, 2009).

11. James T. Madore, "Jobs Head Offshore: Calls About Food Stamps From Needy NYers, Unable to Find Enough Work to Support Families Are Outsourced to Workers in India and Mexico," *NYNewsday.com,* March 5, 2004, 1, http://www.cwalocal4250.org/outsourcing/binary-data/New%20York%20Jobs%20head%20Offshore.pdf (accessed April 21, 2009).

12. Liz Porter, "Why Our Calls, and Jobs, Have Been Delhigated," *The Sunday Age* (July 29, 2001): 2, http://newsstore.theage.com.au/apps/viewDocument.ac?page=1&sy=age&kw=liz+porter&pb=all_ffx&dt=enterRange&dr=10years&sd=01%2F01%2F2000&ed=01%2F01%2F2005&so=date&sf=author&rc=50&rm=200&sp=adv&clsPage=1&docID=SAG010729V88EH5EDTQQ (accessed August 28, 2011).

13. Downey and Fenton, "Global Capital, Local Resistance?": 663.

14. Michael Palm, "Outsourcing, Self-Service and the Telemobility of Work," *Anthropology of Work Review* 27, no. 2 (2006): 1–9, 2.

15. Ibid., 2.

16. Legislation introduced or passed in Congress is cited by year on the website http://www.govtrack.us (accessed August 23, 2011).

17. NFAP, *NFAP Policy Brief,* 6.

18. Ibid., 9.

19. Rosemary Batt, David Holman, and Ursula Holtgrewe, "The Globalization of Service Work: Comparative Institutional Perspectives on Call Centers: Introduction to a Special Issue of ILRR," *Industrial and Labor Relations Review* 62, no. 4 (2009): 453–88, 465.

20. Poster, "Who's on the Line?": 283.

21. Ahmed, *Strange Encounters,* 21. Ahmed uses the term "stranger danger" to refer to the way in which a stranger is understood and embodied as that which needs to be expelled from a community to retain its purity.

22. This description is provided by Downey and Fenton, "Global Capital, Local Resistance?": 659–60. Other images of the pink elephant campaign appear on the CWU Website http://www.cwu.org/11077/news.html (accessed September 1, 2009).

23. Avtar Brah, "Difference, Diversity, Differentiation," in *Feminism and "Race,"* ed. Kum-Kum Bhavnani (Oxford: Oxford University Press, 2001), 456–78.

24. Ahmed, *Strange Encounters,* 3.

25. Senator Wyden, *quoted in* http://www.govtrack.us (accessed on April 21, 2008). While speeches on this bill have been removed from the govtrack.us Website, similar comments by Wyden appear on his Web site, http://beforeitsnews.com/story/52/300/New_Bill_to_Keep_American_Jobs_at_Home.html.

26. Robyn Meredith, "The Next Wave of Offshoring," *Far Eastern Economic Review* 168, no. 3 (March 2005): 1, 5, http://www.feer.com/articles1/2005/0503/free/p019.html (accessed September 1, 2007).

27. Chandra Shekhar, "The Great Indian BPO Scam," *The Financial Express,* July 3, 2006. This article laments the poor enforcement of law in India and reports that 60 percent of

multinational corporations fear that a fraud may occur in India. A number of high-profile cases are described in which employees misused credit card or banking information. See http://www.financialexpress.com/old/latest_full_story.php?content_id = 132637 (accessed September 1, 2007).

28. Richard J. Brennan, "Bell Telemarketers Aggressive, Abusive: CRTC [Canadian Radio-telecom Telecommunications Company] Documents," *The Toronto Star,* January 18, 2011.

29. Radio Canada International, Indo-Canadian Report with Rashi Khilnani, April 20, 2010, http://www.rcinet.ca/english/column/the-indo-canadian-report-with-rashi-khilnani/prejudice-towards-indian-call-centre-workers/.

30. Poster, "Who's on the Line?": 297.

31. As explored further in Chapter 4, local Indian media, business advocates, and workers respond to the outsourcing backlash with a call to Indians to intensify their work productivity.

32. NFAP, *NFAP Policy Brief,* 9, and Downey and Fenton, "Global Capital, Local Resistance?": 664. Downey and Fenton note that discussions on outsourcing in the United Kingdom are frequently situated within discourses of nationalism. Within the "national-liberal" frame, outsourcing is said to benefit the West by providing higher profits and lower consumer costs. In contrast, within the "national-protectionist" frame, outsourcing is seen to harm the nation through job loss and lower quality customer service. In both cases, class distinctions are rarely expressed within these discourses of national interest; for example, rarely is the class of workers who are the real beneficiaries of offshoring acknowledged.

33. Melissa W. Wright, "Asian Spies, American Motors, and Speculations on the Space-Time of Value," *Environment and Planning* 33, no. 12 (2001): 2175–88.

34. Such a perspective where the Western client and customer is conflated reflects the tendency to ignore the class implications of outsourcing. As Downey and Fenton, "Global Capital, Local Resistance?": 657, 663, note, "The benefits for the country that off shores work are not evenly distributed. They accrue primarily to stakeholders and customers. The workers displaced by the off shoring mostly lose out...disagreements that are in reality to do with class interest are either hidden or largely obscured behind the language of nation."

35. Laurie Cohen and Amal El-Sawad, "Accounting for 'Us' and 'Them': Indian and UK Customer Service Workers' Reflections on Offshoring," *Economic and Political Weekly* 42, no. 21 (2007): 1955, http://epw.in/epw/user/userindexHome.jsp (accessed April 21, 2008).

36. Poster's fieldwork corroborates this finding. Poster, "Who's on the Line?": 284.

37. Appadurai, *Modernity at Large,* 42.

38. Rama Lakshmi, "Indian Call Centers Suffer Storm of 4-Letter Words: Executives Blame American Anger Over Outsourcing," *The Washington Post,* February 27, 2005, A22, http://www.washingtonpost.com/ac2/wp-dyn/A56474-2005Feb26?language=printer (accessed September 1, 2008).

39. Sara Ahmed, *Cultural Politics of Emotion,* 15, 43.

40. Arjun Bhardwaj, *Colonial Encounters of a Virtual Kind: The Role of Social Dominance and Situational Factors on Customer Evaluations of Service in Offshore Service Encounters* (doctoral dissertation, University of Western Ontario, 2007). Available from ProQuest Dissertations and Theses database. Bhardwaj studies how customers evaluate offshore service encounters and concludes that customers assume that service provision that originates in India is inferior to service quality from agents within Canada.

41. Ahmed, *Cultural Politics of Emotion,* 60.

42. Arjun Appadurai, *The Fear of Small Numbers: An Essay on the Geography of Anger* (Durham, NC: Duke University Press, 2006), 3. Appadurai traces the links among globalization, violence, and community building. He argues that violence is socially productive in that it provides a concrete, embodied subject toward which citizens within a nation can direct their anxieties toward globalization.

43. Appadurai, *Modernity at Large,* 50.

44. Nira Yuval-Davis, "Women, Globalization and Contemporary Politics of Belonging," *Gender, Technology and Development* 13, no. 1 (2009): 1–19. Yuval-Davis distinguishes belonging from the politics of belonging. The *politics of belonging* involves reproducing the socially sanctioned boundaries between those who belong and those who do not.

4. Surveillance Schooling

1. National Association of Software and Service Companies (NASSCOM), *IT Enabled Services: Background and Reference Resource* (New Delhi, India: NASSCOM, 2001), C28.

2. Sara Ahmed, *Strange Encounters: Embodied Others in Post-Coloniality* (London: Routledge, 2000), 151. Ahmed uses the term "*economy* of difference" to refer to the ways in which the notion of the "strange" is produced, consumed, and exchanged to establish borders around communities.

3. Philomena Essed and David Theo Goldberg, "Cloning Cultures: The Social Injustices of Sameness," *Ethnic and Racial Studies* 25, no. 6 (2002): 1066–82. Essed and Goldberg highlight the social and cultural context that structures the growing interest in determining the genetic composition of food, animals, and even children. They note the broad trend toward cultural cloning, which is the reproduction of preferred types. Underlying cloning is the "normative preference for sameness" (1068). According to Essed and Goldberg, four concepts characterize cloning cultures—kinhood, productivism, consumerism, and aestheticism. The discussion in this chapter traces the ways in which these four dimensions run through discussions of professionalism in Indian call centers. Productivism, consumerism, and aestheticism are ways of building kinhood between India and the West. These cloning cultures simultaneously entrench distinctions between "modern" and "traditional," thereby reproducing the "imperfect sameness" (1067) of India.

4. Ibid., 1075–76. See note 3 above.

5. Shashi Tharoor, "The Coolies are Scheduling the Trains," *Times of India,* April 15, 2007, http://timesofindia.indiatimes.com/home/opinion/shashi-tharoor/shashi-on-sunday/The-coolies-are-scheduling-the-trains/articleshow/1927078.cms (accessed September 1, 2010). Smitha Radhakrishnan, *Appropriately Indian: Gender and Culture in a New Transnational Class* (Durham, NC: Duke University Press, 2011) argues that the new corporate-driven culture is neither Indian nor Western but rather a third global culture. However, as the quotes in this chapter reveal, many respondents experience the new global culture as closely allied to their understandings of Western cultures.

6. Ahmed, *Strange Encounters: Embodied Others in Post-Coloniality* (London: Routledge, 2000), 11.

7. Carol Upadhya, "Management of Culture and Management through Culture in the Indian Software Outsourcing Industry," in *An Outpost of the Global Economy: Work and Workers in India's Information Technology Industry,* ed. C. Upadhya and A. R. Vasavi (New Delhi, India: Routledge, 2008), 101–35. Upadhya's study of the management and training regime in the Indian software industry reveals that Indian software engineers reportedly have a culture of working long hours (they are "sloggers"). Using a cultural justification to justify long work hours hides the fact that this is a requirement posed by many transnational organizations.

8. Shehzad Nadeem, *Dead Ringers: How Outsourcing Is Changing the Way Indians Understand Themselves* (Princeton, NJ: Princeton University Press, 2011), 45.

9. Smitha Radhakrishnan, *Appropriately Indian: Gender and Culture in a New Transnational Class* (Durham, NC: Duke University Press, 2011). Radhakrishnan highlights the class differences between IT (software) and call center workers; the former epitomize the new middle class in India, while the latter are often treated by IT workers as morally suspect due to their nighttime work. IT workers interviewed by Radhakrishnan express uncertainty about whether those

employed at call centers can enact the respectable femininity that is at the core of the streamlined, globally circulated notion of appropriate Indianness. It is clear, however, that call center workers, through their authenticity work, also play a role in reproducing a form of Indianness palatable to Westerners through their daily interactions on the phone.

10. Entry-level customer service agents earn minimum wage in the West (in Canada, this is approximately US$10 per hour, or US$2,000 per month assuming a five-day, ten-hour daily shift. In India, entry-level customer service agents in 2011 working these hours earn between INR 10,000 and INR 20,000 monthly, which converts to US$217–$435 per month). Fieldwork by other researchers corroborates these findings; see, e.g., Diane van den Broek, "Globalising Call Center Capital: Gender, Culture and Work Identity," *Labor & Industry* 14, no. 3 (2004): 59–75; Nadeem, *Dead Ringers* (Princeton, NJ: Princeton University Press, 2011); and Al James and Bhaskar Vira, "'Unionising' the New Spaces of the New Economy? Alternative Labour Organizing in India's IT Enabled Services—Business Process Outsourcing Industry," *Geoforum* 41, no. 3 (2010): 364–76.

11. An attempt was made to contact the organizations mentioned in the advertisements from placement firms described in this chapter. I had hoped to receive copyright permission to reproduce these advertisements. However, none of these agencies responded, and some were not even operational, pointing to the highly volatile nature of this training sector.

12. Company policy document provided by respondent during interview.

13. Julia Evetts, "The Sociological Analysis of Professionalism: Occupational Change in the Modern World," *International Sociology* 18, no 2 (2003): 395–415. Evetts reviews the historical development of the notion of professionalism in the West.

14. Premilla D'Cruz and Ernesto Noronha, "Being Professional: Organizational Control in Indian Call Centers," *Social Science Computer Review* 24, no. 3 (2006): 342–61, 344.

15. Mahuya Pal and Patrice Buzzanell, "The Indian Call Center Experience: A Case Study in Changing Discourses of Identity, Identification and Career in a Global Context," *Journal of Business Communication* 45, no. 1 (2008): 31–60. Pal and Buzzanell study identity construction through participant observation and focus groups at a Kolkata call center. They explore the ways in which workers' identities are far from fixed and are invoked strategically. Workers negotiate their identities through their identity work and their identity at work. They engage in "identity work" when they attempt to define themselves. "Identity at work" is the term used to describe the moment-to-moment interactions with others in which individuals interact in their social contexts, which leads to a reinforcement or shift in the definitions of their identities.

16. Following Essed and Goldberg, "Cloning Cultures," (see note 3 above).

17. Winifred R. Poster, "Who's on the Line? Indian Call Center Agents Pose as Americans for U.S.-Outsourced Firms," *Industrial Relations* 46, no. 2 (2007): 271–304, 285.

18. In a similar way, Nadeem, *Dead Ringers,* 107 argues, "workers construct an image of the West as a social utopia, which is used as a benchmark, a standard against which to measure India's social progress." This can be linked to the civilizing mission as described by Ahmed: "The civilizing mission could be described as a happiness mission. For happiness to be a mission, the colonial other must first be deemed unhappy. . . . It was argued that through empire, the colonized other would acquire good manners, become elevated into a happier state of existence" (Sara Ahmed, "The Politics of Good Feeling," *ACRAWSA—Australian Critical Race and Whiteness Studies Association* 4, no. 1 [2008]: 1–18, 13). Stuart Hall, "The West and the Rest: Discourse and Power," in *Modernity: An Introduction to Modern Societies,* ed. Stuart Hall, David Held, Don Hubert, and Kenneth Thompson (Malden, MA: Blackwell, 1996), 184–227, similarly notes that while the concept of the "West" serves to demarcate the "rest," this "rest" plays an important part in the formation of the idea of the "West." In general, Western spaces are seen as clean and regulated in comparison to "dirty" and "disorderly" (Dipesh Chakrabarty, *Habitations of Modernity: Essays in the Wake of Subaltern Studies* [Chicago: University of Chicago Press, 2002], 76–77). Raka Shome,

"Thinking Through the Diaspora: Call Centers, India, and a New Politics of Hybridity," *International Journal of Cultural Studies* 9, no. 1 (2006): 105–24, describes the physical spaces within which call centers are housed as being "deliberately designed to assert the physicality of a new modernity and cosmopolitanism (read: Americanization) brought about by global technologies, and to distinguish that modernity from the rest of the city (and the nation)" (116). These authors provide further examples of the ways in which the West is defined through equivalences with decency, hygiene, and cleanliness.

19. Essed and Goldberg, "Cloning Cultures," 1069.

20. Shehzad Nadeem, "Macaulay's (Cyber) Children: The Cultural Politics of Outsourcing in India," *Cultural Sociology,* 3 (2009): 102–22, 108.

21. Nadeem, *Dead Ringers,* 142. Nadeem's research similarly reveals that workers are depicted as submissive and deferent. Joint families (where multiple generations live together as one household unit) are seen to be based on frozen feudal relations not conducive to the development of individually oriented, entrepreneurial habits.

22. Diane van den Broek, "Monitoring and Surveillance in Call Centers: Some Responses from Australian Workers," *Labor & Industry* 12, no. 3 (2002): 43–58, 49–50.

23. Taylorism refers to the scientific management method developed by Frederick W. Taylor in the early 1900s which involved the separation of jobs into discrete repetitive tasks. In a similar way, calls were broken down into segments (for example, opening, answering questions, selling, closing, and so forth), and workers were asked to read from computer screens that provided exact scripts or script notes.

24. Laurie Cohen and Amal El-Sawad, "Accounting for 'Us' and 'Them': Indian and UK Customer Service Workers' Reflections on Offshoring," *Economic and Political Weekly* 42, no. 21 (2007): 1951–57, 1955, http://epw.in/epw/user/userindexHome.jsp (accessed April 21, 2009).

25. Robin Leidner, "Emotional Labor in Service Work," *Annals of the American Academy of Political and Social Science* 561, no. 1 (1999): 81–95. Leidner provides the example of McDonald's employees who willingly accept routinization because it allows them to maintain their distance and self-esteem in response to customer mistreatment: "[U]nder some conditions, scripted emotional labour can help workers enforce their will over others, protect themselves from mistreatment, bolster their confidence in their abilities, or at least offer them some psychological distance from disagreeable interactions" (93).

26. Monica Heller, "Language, Skill and Authenticity in the Globalized New Economy," *Noves SL. Revista de Sociolingüística* Winter (2005): 107, http://www6.gencat.cat/llengcat/noves/hm05hivern/docs/heller.pdf (accessed September 1, 2005). Heller identifies two contradictory trends in service work—professionalism and quality. *Professionalism* justifies the need for the standardization of service that is achieved through surveillance, measurement, and control over work. *Quality,* however, depends on the authenticity and adaptability of workers.

27. Rosemary Batt, David Holman, and Ursula Holtgrewe, "The Globalization of Service Work: Comparative Institutional Perspectives on Call Centers: Introduction to a Special Issue of ILRR," *Industrial and Labor Relations Review* 62, no. 4 (2009): 453–88; Rosemary Batt, Virginia Doellgast, Hyunji Kwon, Mudit Nopany, Priti Nopany, and Anil da Costa, "The Indian Call Center Industry: National Benchmarking Report Strategy, HR Practices, & Performance," *CAHRS Working Paper Series* (no. 7) (Ithaca, NY: Cornell University, School of Industrial and Labor Relations, Center for Advanced Human Resource Studies, 2005), http://digitalcommons.ilr.cornell.edu/cahrswp/7 (accessed September 1, 2005), note that a majority of workers in India have little discretion to handle customer complaints or unexpected requests. At the same time, U.S. call center workers are required to rely more heavily on scripts than agents in India.

28. Bob Russell, *Smiling Down the Line: Info-Service Work in the Global Economy* (Toronto: University of Toronto Press, 2009). Russell notes the "recombination" of info-service work [ITES

jobs] where there is an increase in the job span. The growing complexity of work is accompanied by the development of new managerial practices.

29. In a study on why a British bank closed its call center in India, Angela Coyle, "'Are You in This Country?' How 'Local' Social Relations Can Limit the Globalization of Customer Services Supply Chains," *Antipode* 42, no. 2 (2010): 289–309, notes that Indians are said to lack the confidence to "go off the script." This caused enormous customer backlash.

30. Catrina Alferoff and David Knights, "We're All Partying Here: Target and Games, or Targets as Games in Call Center Management," in *Art and Aesthetics at Work*, ed. Adrian Carr and Philip Hancock (Basingstoke, England: Palgrave Macmillan, 2003), 70–92. New forms of monitoring include indirect control through competition and rewards.

31. Donald J. Winiecki, "The Call Center and Its Many Players," *Organization* 16 (2009), 705–31. Drawing on actor network theory, Winiecki describes the emergence of a central figure—"qualictivity" (focus on quality scores)—in call center organizations. This "non-living actor" interacts with living actors (workers, managers, trainers) who fashion themselves so they can be captured in quality scores. In this way, quality assessments become the "master choreographer" of work in a call center.

32. Diane van den Broek, G. Callaghan, and P. Thompson, "Teams Without Teamwork? Explaining the Call Center Paradox," *Economic and Industrial Democracy* 25, no. 2 (2004): 197–218, 211. Teams serve primarily to motivate employees and challenge the isolation of call center work.

33. Homi K. Bhabha, *The Location of Culture* (London: Routledge, 1994). Bhabha's notion of mimicry is an important one to understand the managerial strategies in Indian call centers. Bhabha characterizes *mimicry* as a colonial desire and an effective strategy of colonial power. It is the wish to create knowable notions of the Other. Mimicry "appropriates the Other as it visualizes power" (126). Insofar as this visualization is never complete, mimicry produces a slippage. This slippage authenticates the power of the colonizer because the Other is never quite the same, but it also disrupts the authority of the colonizer, allowing the possibility of self-determination of the Other.

34. Nadeem, *Dead Ringers*, 94.

35. John M. Jermier, David Knights, and Walter R. Nord, "Resistance and Power in Organizations: Agency, Subjectivity and the Labor Process," in *Resistance and Power in Organizations*, ed. John M. Jermier, David Knights, and Walter R. Nord (London: Routledge, 1994), 1–24, for example, argue that the de-skilling of work or the downgrading of the employee experience can be accompanied by attempts to sabotage and resist the imposition of capitalist control strategies. Diane Van Den Broek, "Monitoring and Surveillance in Call Centers: Some Responses from Australian Workers," *Labor & Industry* 12, no. 3 (2002): 43–58, terms the forms of resistance used by call center workers as "flicking." She describes flicking strategies utilized by workers in Australian call centers, such as hanging up on customers, redirecting calls, leaving customers waiting, or putting customers back into the queue (55). In a similar vein, Carla Freeman, *High Tech and High Heels in the Global Economy: Women, Work, and Pink-Collar Identities in the Caribbean* (Durham, NC: Duke University Press, 2000), shows how informatics workers in the Caribbean "trick" the system to lighten the load of their production quotas by finding glitches in the computer monitoring system; "these incidents reveal a degree of ingenuity and understanding of the labor process and the technology which directly challenges the 'closed-system' design of these jobs" (210). Garima Kumar and Anand Prakash, "Interplay of Management Control, and Employee Agency in a Call Centre," *Indian Journal of Industrial Relations* 43, no. 4 (2008): 574–602, provide examples of workers' use of humor and sarcasm to challenge management agendas at a large call center based in Gurgaon, India.

36. As Heidi Gottfried, "Learning the Score: The Duality of Control and Everyday Resistance in the Temporary-Help Service Industry," in *Resistance and Power in Organizations*, ed. John M. Jermier, David Knights, and Walter R. Nord (London: Routledge, 1994), 102–27, argues, "[T]he possibilities for more illicit, subterranean forms of resistance like sabotage and theft

have been enhanced by computerization giving workers the ability to shut down entire systems with minimal effort" (120). Freeman, *High Tech and High Heels* (Durham, NC: Duke University Press, 2000), notes that "workers cleverly manipulate a tool that by design is meant to elude their understanding" (210).

37. Diane Van den Broek, Alison Barnes, and Keith Townsend, "'Teaming up': Teams and Team Sharing in Call Centers," *Journal of Industrial Relations* 50, no. 2 (2008): 257–69. Van den Broek refers to this process as "teaming up," whereby team members can provide collective support for one another despite the competitive structure of teams.

38. Arjun Appadurai, "Grassroots Globalization and the Research Imagination," *Public Culture* 12, no. 1 (2000): 1–19, 5.

39. Leela Fernandes, "The Politics of Forgetting: Class Politics, State Power and the Restructuring of Urban Space in India," *Urban Studies* 41, no. 12 (2004): 2415–30. Fernandes historicizes the emergence of India's new middle class as a social group. She notes that while this class is highly visible, it involves a "politics of forgetting" the uneven impact of globalization, which has involved cultural-spatial purification and mass dislocation (2418–19).

40. Mathangi Krishnamurthy, "Resources and Rebels: A Study of Identity Management in Indian Call Centers," *Anthropology of Work Review* 25, nos. 3–4 (2004): 9–18, 11.

41. Celia V. Harquail, "Employees as Animate Artifacts: Employee Branding by 'Wearing the Brand,'" in *Artifacts and Organizations: Beyond Mere Symbolism,* ed. Anat Rafaeil and Michael G. Pratt (Mahwah, NJ: Lawrence Erlbaum, 2006), 161–80, 170–71.

42. Garima Kumar and Anand Prakash, "Interplay of Management Control and Employee Agency in a Call Centre," *Indian Journal of Industrial Relations* 43, no. 4 (2008): 574–602. This is based on an organizational ethnography of team-and-culture-building exercises being used in a large call center in Gurgaon, India.

43. Peter Fleming, *Authenticity and the Cultural Politics of Work: New Forms of Informal Control* (Oxford: Oxford University Press, 2009), 57, 59, 70.

44. Sareeta Amrute, "Living and Praying the Code: The Flexibility and Discipline of Indian Information Technology Workers (ITers) in a Global Economy," *Anthropological Quarterly* 83, no. 3 (2010): 519–50.

45. Other researchers corroborate these findings. As Alferoff and Knights, "We're All Partying Here," 70–92, note, "targets, incentives and comparative performances are shrouded in game-like competitions and contests that are intended to transform productivity pursuits into an exercise of fun" (76). Krishnamurthy, "Resources and Rebels," argues that "there is an inherent paradox in demanding professionalism from workers hired on the incentive of 'fun'" (15).

46. Reena Patel, *Working the Night Shift: Women in India's Call Center Industry* (Palo Alto, CA: Stanford University Press, 2010), 43. Patel recounts the experience of one woman who pays two thousand rupees for a company-initiated social trip every three months.

47. As Samuel Bowles and Herbert Gintis, *Schooling in Capitalist America: Educational Reform and the Contradictions of Economic Life* (New York: Basic Books, 1976), note, "[S]chools foster types of personal development compatible with the relationships of dominance and subordinacy in the economic sphere" (11). For other examples of ways in which the cultures of schooling pervade call centers in India, see Winifred R. Poster, "Saying 'Good Morning' in the Night: The Reversal of Work Time in Global ICT Service Work," in *Research in the Sociology of Work* 17 (2007): 78; Tina J. K. Basi, *Women, Identity and India's Call Center Industry* (London: Routledge, 2009), 69.

48. Peter McLaren, "Schooling the Postmodern Body: Critical Pedagogy and the Politics of Enfleshment," *Journal of Education* 170, no. 1 (1988): 53–83, 63, *cited in* Nirmala Erevelles, "Educating Unruly Bodies: Critical Pedagogy, Disability Studies, and the Politics of Schooling," *Educational Theory* 50, no. 1 (2000): 25–47, 33.

49. Bowles and Gintis, *Schooling in Capitalist America,* 11. As Bowles and Gintis note, schools socialize working class and poor youth to accept individual responsibility for the conditions of

their poverty and thus locate the source of economic failure in individuals rather that in the social and economic structure of capitalism. This socialization often reproduces social difference along the lines of race.

50. Nadeem, "Macaulay's (Cyber) Children," 119.

51. Poster, "Who's on the Line?": 282.

5. "Don't Take Calls, Make Contact!"

1. Lior Arussy, "Don't Take Calls, Make Contact," *Harvard Business Review* 80, no. 1 (2002): 16, http://hbr.org/2002/01/dont-take-calls-make-contact/ar/1 (accessed January 2, 2003).

2. Robert Miles, *Racism* (London: Routledge, 1989), 75. Miles defines *racialization* as a "process of categorization" through which "social relations between people [are] structured by the signification of human biological characteristics in such a way as to define and construct differentiated social collectivities." Notions of "Self" and "Other" continually inform the relations of production within which call center work is situated.

3. This resonates with Sandra Acker and Michelle Webber, "Pleasure and Danger in Academics' Feelings About Their Work" (paper presented at the American Educational Research Association, New Orleans, LA, April 24–28, 2000). They observed that "in today's organizing for globalization, we can see the emergence of a hegemonic hyper-masculinity that is aggressive, ruthless, competitive and adversarial" (29).

4. David Theo Goldberg, *The Threat of Race: Reflections on Racial Neoliberalism* (Malden, MA: Wiley-Blackwell, 2009). Goldberg shows how racial preferences can be freely exercised as individual choice in neoliberalism. The state supports this privatization of race because the private sphere is valorized as a space free from state intervention. Given that customer service calls often occur from customers' homes—the quintessential private space—customers are free to make racist remarks as a way of expressing their consumer preference.

5. Leslie Salzinger, *Genders in Production: Making Workers in Mexico's Global Factories* (Berkeley: University of California Press, 2003), 12. As Jill Steans also notes in "The Gender Dimension," in *The Global Transformation Reader: An Introduction to the Globalization Debate,* ed. David Held and Anthony G. McGrew (Cambridge: Polity Press, 2003), "in Asia, in the 1980s, women made up 85 per cent of workers in Export Production Zones. In other areas, the figure for women workers was typically around 75 per cent" (368).

6. Aihwa Ong, "The Gender and Labor Politics of Postmodernity," *Annual Review of Anthropology* 20 (1991): 279–309, 287.

7. These figures have been identified by Steans, "The Gender Dimension," in *The Global Transformation Reader* (Cambridge: Polity Press, 2003), 368. Other theorists who trace the ideological construction of appropriate jobs for women include Salzinger, *Genders in Production;* Suzanne Bergeron, "Political Economy Discourses of Globalization and Feminist Politics," *Signs* 26, no. 4 (2001): 983–1006; Victoria Carty, "Ideologies and Forms of Domination in the Organization of the Global Production and Consumption of Goods in the Emerging Postmodern Era: A Case Study of Nike Corporation and the Implications for Gender," *Gender, Work and Organization* 4, no. 4 (1997): 189–201; Ong, "Gender and Labor Politics"; Robin Leidner, "Serving Hamburgers and Selling Insurance: Gender, Work, and Identity in Interactive Service Jobs, *Gender & Society* 5, no. 2 (1991): 154–77; see also Lisa Adkins, *Gendered Work: Sexuality, Family and the Labor Market* (Buckingham, England: Open University Press, 1995); Donald Tomaskovic-Devey, *Gender & Racial Inequality at Work: The Sources & Consequences of Job Segregation* (Ithaca, NY: Cornell University Press, 1993).

8. Amrita Basu, Inderpal Grewal, Caren Kaplan, and Lisa Malkki, "Editorial," *Signs* 26, no. 4 (2001): 943–48, 943.

9. Meera Nanda, "Post-Fordist Technology and the Changing Patterns of Women's Employment in the Third World," *Gender, Technology and Development* 4, no. 1 (2000): 25–59, 26. Salzinger,

Genders in Production, similarly documents the growing integration of men into the maquiladoras through a case study of a factory that employs an equal number of women and men.

10. The exact gender breakdown of the industry is difficult to pinpoint. Advait Aundhkar, Nalini Vaz, Gita A. Pillai, D. L. N. Murthy, S. S. Thakar, and Sujata Gothoskar, "Nature of Teleworking in Key Sectors: Case Studies of Financial, Media and Software Sectors in Mumbai," *Economic and Political Weekly* 35, no. 26 (June 24, 2000): 2277–92, http://epw.in/epw/user/userindexHome.jsp (accessed April 21, 2005), note that between 40 percent and 70 percent of call center workers are women. Cecilia Ng and Swasti Mitter, "Valuing Women's Voices: Call Center Workers in Malaysia and India," *Gender, Technology and Development* 9, no. 2 (2005): 209–33, argue that 45 percent of employees on the payrolls of call centers in India are women. Sanjukta Mukherjee, *Producing the IT Miracle: The Neoliberalizing States and Changing Gender and Class Regimes in India* (doctoral dissertation, Syracuse University, 2008) (available from ProQuest Dissertations and Theses database, notes that there are more women in IT/ITES jobs in India than in any other sector, although women are more present in call centers than software firms. Similar findings are presented by Marisa D'Mello, "'Are You Married?' Exploring Gender in a Global Workplace in India," in *Work and Life in the Global Economy: A Gendered Analysis of Service Work,* ed. Debra Howcroft and Helen Richardson (New York: Palgrave Macmillan, 2010), 52–77. State and state-allied organizations overtly promote technology work as gender neutral (Carol Upadhya, "Gender Issues in the Indian Software Outsourcing Industry," in *Gender in the Information Society: Emerging Issues,* ed. A. Gurumurthy, P. J. Singh, A. Mundkur, and M. Swamy [New Delhi, India: Elsevier, 2006], 74–84.) This sector in India provides better-paid jobs than local centers or those providing telemarketing and data-processing services. Women also tend to predominate in these latter types of jobs (Govind Kelkar, Girija Shrestha, and N. Veena, "IT Industry and Women's Agency: Explorations in Bangalore and Delhi, India," *Gender, Technology and Development* 6, no. 1 [2002]: 63–84).

11. Yvonne Benschop and Hans Doorewaard, "Covered by Equality: The Gender Subtext of Organizations," *Organization Studies* 19, no. 5 (1998): 787–805, use the term "subtext" to refer to "the set of often concealed, power-based gendering processes, i.e. organizational and individual arrangements (objectives, measures, habits), systematically (re)producing gender distinctions" (787).

12. Lisa Adkins, "Cultural Feminization: "Money, Sex and Power" for Women," *Signs* 26, no. 3 (2001): 669–95, 680.

13. Donna Haraway, *Simians, Cyborgs and Women: The Reinvention of Nature* (New York; Routledge, 1991), 149–181, *quoted in* Lisa Adkins and Eeva Jokinen, "Introduction: Gender, Living and Labor in the Fourth Shift," *NORA—Nordic Journal of Feminist and Gender Research* 16, no. 3 (2008): 138–49, 138.

14. Salzinger, *Genders in Production,* 15.

15. Ibid., 36.

16. Deborah Cameron, "Styling the Worker: Gender and the Commodification of Language in the Globalized Service Economy, *Journal of Sociolinguistics* 4, no. 3 (2000): 323–47, 335. Garima Kumar and Anand Prakash, "Interplay of Management Control and Employee Agency in a Call Centre," *Indian Journal of Industrial Relations* 43, no. 4 (2008): 574–602, make a similar argument.

17. Some theorists writing on emotion work include Jane Aronson and Sheila M. Neysmith, "'You're Not Just in There to Do the Work': Depersonalizing Policies and the Exploitation of Home Care Workers' Labor," *Gender & Society* 10, no. 1 (1996): 59–77; Jaber F. Gubrium, "Emotion Work and Emotive Discourse in the Alzheimer's Disease Experience," *Current Perspectives on Aging and the Life Cycle* 3 (1989): 243–68; Carol A. Heimer and Mitchell L. Stevens, "Caring for the Organization: Social Workers as Frontline Risk Managers in Neonatal Intensive Care Units," *Work and Occupations* 24, no. 2 (1997): 133–63; Arlie Russell Hochschild, *The Managed Heart: Commercialization of Human Feeling* (Berkeley: University of California Press, 1983); Jennifer L. Pierce, *Gender Trials: Emotional Lives in Contemporary Law Firms* (Berkeley: University of California Press, 1995); Anat Rafaeli and Robert I. Sutton, "Emotional Contrast Strategies as

Means of Social Influence: Lessons from Criminal Interrogators and Bill Collectors," *Academy of Management Journal* 34, no. 4 (1991): 749–75, http://journals.aomonline.org/amj/ (accessed April 21, 2002); John Van Maanen and Giedon Kunda, "'Real Feelings': Emotional Expression and Organizational Culture," *Research in Organizational Behavior* 11 (1989): 43–103.

18. For a detailed review of this literature, see Kiran Mirchandani, "Challenging Racial Silences in Studies of Emotion Work: Contributions from Anti-Racist Feminist Theory," *Organization Studies* 24, no. 5 (2003): 721–42. Arlie Russell Hochschild, "Emotion Work, Feeling Rules, and Social Structure," *American Journal of Sociology* 85, no. 3 (1979): 551–75, terms emotion work done for a wage as "emotion labor" and defines this as "the act of trying to change in degree or quality an emotion or feeling" (561). Stephen Fineman, "Emotion and Organizing," in *Handbook of Organization Studies,* ed. Stewart R. Clegg, Cynthia Hardy, and Walter R. Nord (London: Sage, 1996), 543–64, notes that "emotional 'labor' is the buying of an employee's emotional demeanor; the individual is being paid to 'look nice,' smile, be caring, be polite" (546). The emotion labor of flight attendants thus involves "trying to feel the right feeling for the job" (Hochschild, *The Managed Heart,* 118). Bill collectors do emotion labor to deflate customers' status and evoke gratitude or fear in clients (Hochschild, *The Managed Heart*), 138. Emotion work involves managing feelings as well as defining one's work. Bonalyn J. Nelsen and Stephen R. Barley, "For Love or Money? Commodification and the Construction of an Occupational Mandate," *Administrative Science Quarterly* 42, no. 4 (1997): 619–53, http://www.johnson.cornell.edu/publications/asq/ (accessed April 21, 2002), for example, examine the emotion work of paid and volunteer emergency medical systems personnel. While paid workers emphasize the highly skilled, commodifiable qualities of emergency medical work, volunteers stressed the humanitarian and caring nature of the same work. Gary Alan Fine, "Justifying Work: Occupational Rhetorics as Resources in Restaurant Kitchens," *Administrative Science Quarterly* 41, no. 1 (1996): 90–115, http://www.johnson.cornell.edu/publications/asq/ (accessed April 21, 2002), in a similar way, demonstrates the strategies used by restaurant cooks to define their work as worthy of respect and professionalization.

19. Cameron Lynne Macdonald and Carmen J. Sirianni, eds., *Working in the Service Society* (Philadelphia: Temple University Press, 1996). Macdonald and Sirianni use this term to refer to the class differences among the service workforce.

20. Jeff Hearn, "Feeling Out of Place? Towards the Transnationalizations of Emotions," in *The Emotional Organization: Passions and Power,* ed. Stephen Fineman (Malden, MA: Blackwell, 2008), 184–201, 197.

21. Drucilla K. Barker and Susan F. Feiner, "Affect, Race, and Class: An Interpretive Reading of Caring Labor," *Frontiers: A Journal of Women's Studies* 30, no. 1 (2009):41–45.

22. This description is provided by a training manager interviewed by Kumar and Prakash, "Interplay of Management Control," 587.

23. Given the structure of production, Marek Korczynski, "Communities of Coping: Collective Emotional Labor in Service Work," *Organization* 10, no. 1 (2003): 55–79, argues that "the irate and abusive customer should be seen as a systematic part of the social relations of service work" (57).

24. Winifred R. Poster, "Who's on the line? Indian Call Center Agents Pose as Americans for U.S.-Outsourced Firms," *Industrial Relations* 46, no. 2 (2007): 271–304, 282.

25. As Phil Taylor, Premilla D'Cruz, Ernesto Noronha, and Dora Scholarios, "Domestic Labour: The Experience of Work in India's Other Call Centre Industry," in *Work and Life in the Global Economy: A Gendered Analysis of Service Work,* ed. Debra Howcroft and Helen Richardson (New York: Palgrave Macmillan, 2010), 99–123, note, Indian call centers are often managed via corporate decisions made in the West. In this context, it is important to situate understandings of Indian call centers within the context of events and trends in the West.

26. Joan Acker, "Gender, Capitalism and Globalization," *Critical Sociology* 30, no. 1 (2004): 17–41, 31.

27. Marek Korczynski and Ursula Ott, "When Production and Consumption Meet: Cultural Contradictions and the Enchanting Myth of Customer Sovereignty," *Journal of Management*

Studies 41, no. 4 (2004): 575–99, 580–81. See also Marek Korczynski and Vicky Bishop, "Abuse, Violence, and Fear on the Front Line: Implications for the Rise of the Enchanting Myth of Customer Sovereignty," in *The Emotional Organization: Passions and Power,* ed. Stephen Fineman (Malden, MA: Blackwell, 2008), 74–87.

28. Permilla D'Cruz and Ernesto Noronha, "Experiencing Depersonalized Bullying: A Study of Indian Call-Center Agents," in *Working at the Interface: Call-Center Labor in a Global Economy,* ed. Ursula Huws (London, England: Analytica, 2009), 26–46, 26. With regard to the normalized and generalized nature of abuse in service work, Korczynski and Bishop, "Abuse, Violence, and Fear," note that within the ideology of customer sovereignty, abuse is seen as a normal and legitimate customer response, requiring little management or legislative sanction, and victims are encouraged to see abuse as a result of their own failings to perform their jobs. As a result, everyday abuse and violence is routinized (76).

29. Korczynski and Bishop, "Abuse, Violence, and Fear," 83–84.

30. Vicky Bishop, Marek Korczynski, and Laurie Cohen, "The Invisibility of Violence: Constructing Violence out of the Job Center Workplace in the UK," *Work, Employment and Society* 19, no. 3 (2005): 583–602, 586.

31. Masculinity can also structure work expectations. Darren Nixon, "'I Can't Put a Smiley Face On': Working-Class Masculinity, Emotional Labor and Service Work in the 'New Economy,'" *Gender, Work and Organization* 16, no. 3 (2009): 300–22, notes that particular forms of masculinity, such as that of working-class men, are antithetical to service work because this kind of work requires deference and docility. Working-class masculinity involves "sticking up for yourself, speaking your mind and 'fronting up' when challenged" (310).

32. This is one of the ways in which professionalism is defined in call centers, as shown by D'Cruz and Noronha, "Experiencing Depersonalized Bullying."

33. Cameron Lynne Macdonald and David Merrill, "Intersectionality in the Emotional Proletariat: A New Lens on Employment Discrimination in Service Work," in *Service Work: Critical Perspectives,* ed. Cameron Lynne Macdonald and Marek Korczynski (New York: Routledge, 2009), 113–33, 125.

34. Korczynski and Bishop, "Abuse, Violence, and Fear," 75.

35. Korczynski and Ott, "Production and Consumption Meet," 590. Korczynski and Ott use the term "asymmetrical grammar" to refer to the structural inequality between service provider and service recipient.

36. Goldberg, *The Threat of Race,* 363.

37. Philomena Essed, *Understanding Everyday Racism: An Interdisciplinary Theory* (Newbury Park, CA: Sage, 1991). Essed uses the term "everyday racism" to refer to racial practices. These are implicit racial assumptions that structure seemingly race-neutral social behaviors.

38. Bob Russell, *Smiling Down the Line: Info-Service Work in the Global Economy* (Toronto: University of Toronto Press, 2009). Russell notes that customer service work involves an exchange among managers, workers, and customers. Given the key role played by customers in interactions, there is always an element of variability and uncertainty in customer service work, 93.

39. Korczynski and Bishop, "Abuse, Violence, and Fear," 74.

40. NIIT, *Certificate in Customer Service: Student Guide-I* (New Delhi, India: Sona Printers, 2003), 5.5, 3.6.

41. Bishop, Korczynski, and Cohen, "The Invisibility of Violence," 594–95.

42. Tina J. K. Basi, *Women, Identity and India's Call Center Industry* (London: Routledge, 2009), 159.

43. Sharon C. Bolton and Maeve Houlihan, "Risky Business: Re-Thinking the Human in Interactive Service Work," in *Searching for the Human in Human Resource Management: Theory, Practice and Workplace Contexts,* ed. Sharon C. Bolton and Maeve Houlihan (Basingstoke, England: Palgrave Macmillan, 2007), 245–62, 246.

44. Ibid., 246.

6. Being Nowhere in the World

1. Barbara Adam, *Timescapes of Modernity: The Environment and Invisible Hands* (London: Routledge, 1998), 17. Adam notes that "with the globalization of clock time, all that is local, context-specific, dependent, and seasonal becomes an obstacle to be overcome," 17.

2. Ibid., 14. Adam also uses the term "colonization with time" to refer to the way in which Western clock time is seen as the universal standard (21).

3. Barbara Adam, "The Gendered Time Politics of Globalization: Of Shadowlands and Elusive Justice," *Feminist Review* 70 (2002): 3–29, 18, http://www.feminist-review.com (accessed January 31, 2003).

4. Vinay Lal, *Empire of Knowledge: Culture and Plurality in the Global Economy* (London: Pluto Press, 2002), 19. Lal traces the ways in which the "lazy native" was historically constructed in colonial discourse as lacking appropriate time habits.

5. Shehzad Nadeem, "The Uses and Abuses of Time: Globalization and Time Arbitrage in India's Outsourcing Industries," *Global Networks* 9, no. 1 (2008): 20–40, 25.

6. Winifred R. Poster, "Saying 'Good Morning' in the Night: The Reversal of Work Time in Global ICT Service Work," *Research in the Sociology of Work* 17 (2007): 77.

7. Ibid., 85.

8. Adam, *Timescapes of Modernity,* 1.

9. Poster, "Saying 'Good Morning' in the Night," 105.

10. Reena Patel, *Working the Night Shift: Women in India's Call Center Industry* (Palo Alto, CA: Stanford University Press, 2010); and Sanjukta Mukherjee, *Producing the IT Miracle: The Neoliberalizing States and Changing Gender and Class Regimes in India* (doctoral dissertation, Syracuse University, 2008) (available from ProQuest Dissertations and Theses database) have also identified this trend.

11. Naila Kabeer, "Marriage, Motherhood and Masculinity in the Global Economy: Reconfigurations of Personal and Economic Life," *Institute of Development Studies Working Paper 290* (Brighton, England: University of Sussex, 2007).

12. Preeti Singh and Anu Pandey, "Women in Call Centres," *Economic and Political Weekly* 40, no. 7 (2005): 684–88, 687. Also Rekha Pande, "Looking at Information Technology from a Gender Perspective: The Call Centers in India," *Asian Journal of Women's Studies* 11, no. 1 (2005): 58–82. Pande's interviews with fifty call center workers in Hydrabad reveal that married women continued to have significant domestic and childcare responsibilities but "had little time to take charge of their homes and hence decisions were primarily taken by men or others in the family who were at home" (77).

13. Babu P. Ramesh, "Cyber Coolies in BPO: Insecurities and Vulnerabilities of Non-Standard Work," *Economic and Political Weekly* 39, no. 5 (2004): 492–97, 497.

14. Claire Williams, *Blue, White and Pink Collar Workers: Technicians, Bank Employees and Flight Attendants* (London: Allen Unwin, 1988), quoted in Lisa Adkins, *Gendered Work: Sexuality, Family and the Labor Market* (Buckingham, England: Open University Press, 1995), 10.

15. Patel, *Working the Night Shift,* 35. Patel defines these as norms that dictate what women can and cannot do. By working at night, women risk being perceived as morally lacking given the expectation that respectable women do not occupy the urban nightspace.

16. In 2008, a local radio station (Radio Mirchi) and other news media reported that an AIDS control society had recommended the installation of condom vending machines in call centers.

17. Shelly Tara and P. Ilavarasan Vigneswara, "'I Would Not Have Been Working Here!' Parental Support to Unmarried Daughters as Call Center Agents in India," *Gender, Technology and Development* 13, no. 3 (2009): 385–406, 399.

18. Winifred R. Poster, "Dangerous Places and Nimble Fingers: Discourses of Gender Discrimination and Rights in Global Corporations," *International Journal of Politics, Culture, and Society* 15, no. 1 (2001): 77–105. Poster describes the ways in which the rhetoric of dangerous places is often used to exclude women from jobs that are seen as too hazardous for women.

19. Joan Acker, "Gender, Capitalism and Globalization," *Critical Sociology* 30, no. 1 (2004): 17–41, 27.

20. Petlee Peter, "Reckless Driving by Call Centre Drivers Poses Threat to Others," *The Hindu,* September 22, 2008, 2, http://www.hindu.com/2008/09/14/stories/2008091452390300.htm (accessed August 24, 2011).

21. Chandran Iyer, "BPO Rape: Police Still Clueless," *Midday,* August 25, 2008, http://www.mid-day.com/news/2008/aug/250808-gang-rape-call-center-employee-culprit-not-nabbed.htm. (accessed April 21, 2009).

22. Reena Patel, "Working the Night Shift: Gender and the Global Economy," *ACME: An International E-Journal for Critical Geographies* 5, no. 1 (2006): 9–27, 14, http://www.acme-journal.org/index.html (accessed April 21, 2007).

23. Shehzad Nadeem, *Dead Ringers: How Outsourcing Is Changing the Way Indians Understand Themselves* (Princeton, NJ: Princeton University Press, 2011), 96.

24. David Harvey, *The Condition of Postmodernity: An Enquiry into the Origins of Cultural Change* (Malden, MA: Blackwell, 1989), 306. Harvey refers to the ways in which globalization leads to a reduction in spatial and temporal distances.

25. Cindi Katz, "On the Grounds of Globalization: A Topography for Feminist Political Engagement," *Signs* 26, no. 4 (2001): 1213–34. In her ethnography of the effects of global restructuring in a village called Howa in Sudan, Katz explains, "from the vantage point of capital, the world may be shrinking, but, on the marooned grounds of places such as Howa, it appeared to be getting bigger every day" (1224). With the out-migration of men from Howa, there was a much higher reliance on the labor of children, who had to travel long hours for wood gathering, making their school attendance difficult. As a result, children did not have the opportunity to develop the skills necessary to participate in the new global economy from which they were further disconnected.

26. Winifred R. Poster, "Saying 'Good Morning' in the Night: The Reversal of Work Time in Global ICT Service Work," in *Research in the Sociology of Work* 17 (2007): 97, notes that "while the state has stepped forward to aid politically and financially the entrepreneurs who created the night time city, it has withdrawn from the citizens who work in it."

27. Ursula Huws, ed., "Working at the Interface: Call-Center Labor in a Global Economy," in *Working at the Interface: Call-Center Labor in a Global Economy* (London: Analytica, 2009), 1–8, 3.

28. Lisa Adkins, "Feminism after Measure," *Feminist Theory* 10, no. 3 (2009): 323–39, 330.

29. Carol Upadhya, "Gender Issues in the Indian Software Outsourcing Industry," in *Gender in the Information Society: Emerging Issues,* ed. Anita Gurumurthy, Parminder Jeet Singh, Anu Mundkur, and Mridula Swamy (New Delhi, India: Elsevier, 2006), 74–84, http://www.apdip.net/publications/ict4d/GenderIS.pdf (accessed April 21, 2007). Upadhya uses the term "discursive gymnastics" to refer to the strategies used by managers to reconcile the construction of software work as gender neutral and woman-friendly, alongside expectations of highly masculine work times and norms that hinder the full participation of women. Managers place responsibility for gender imbalance on women's failure to be entrepreneurial and work long hours.

30. Ratna Sudarshan, *Gender Statistics and Development Policy: Women's Work in India* (Paris: Organisation for Economic Co-operation and Development [OECD], 2009), http://www.oecd.org/dataoecd/22/10/41746107.pps [PowerPoint presentation] (accessed June 21, 2011). Sudarshan notes that women in India spend an average of thirty-five hours and men four hours per week on care and household maintenance.

Conclusion

1. Theorists who have analyzed these forms of labor include: Lisa Adkins, "Feminism after Measure," *Feminist Theory* 10, no. 3 (2009): 323–39. Arlene C. Daniels, "Invisible Work," *Social Problems* 34 (1987): 403–15; Nona Y. Glazer, *Women's Paid and Unpaid Labour: The Work Transfer of*

Health Care and Retailing (Philadelphia: Temple University Press, 1993); Arlie Russell Hochschild, *The Managed Heart: Commercialization of Human Feeling* (Berkeley: University of California Press, 1983); Bob Russell, *Smiling Down the Line: Info-Service Work in the Global Economy* (Toronto: University of Toronto Press, 2009); Carol Wolkowitz, *Bodies at Work* (London: Sage, 2006).

2. Rosemary Batt, Virginia Doellgast, Hyunji Kwon, Mudit Nopany, Priti Nopany, and Anil da Costa, "The Indian Call Center Industry: National Benchmarking Report Strategy, HR Practices, & Performance," *CAHRS Working Paper Series* (no. 7) (Ithaca, NY: Cornell University, School of Industrial and Labor Relations, Center for Advanced Human Resource Studies, 2005), 465, http://digitalcommons.ilr.cornell.edu/cahrswp/7 (accessed September 1, 2007).

3. Rosemary Batt, David Holman, and Ursula Holtgrewe, "The Globalization of Service Work: Comparative Institutional Perspectives on Call Centers: Introduction to a Special Issue of ILRR," *Industrial and Labor Relations Review* 62, no. 4 (2009): 453–88.

4. Charles Guignon "Authenticity," *Philosophy Compass* 3, no. 2 (2008): 277–90.

5. This is one example of the importance of authenticity claims; see http://www.aboriginalartshop.com (accessed on September 1, 2010).

6. Richard A. Peterson, "In Search of Authenticity," *Journal of Management Studies* 42, no. 5 (2005): 1083–98. Peterson identifies three ways in which authenticity is claimed: through ethnic/cultural identity (one's right to represent the group to which one is seen to ethnically belong), through status identity, and through constructed self.

7. Ibid.,1086.

8. Jaber F. Gubrium and James A. Holstein, "The Everyday Work and Auspices of Authenticity," in *Authenticity in Culture, Self, and Society,* ed. Phillip Vannini and J. Patrick Williams (Farnham, England: Ashgate, 2009), 121–39, 123.

9. Ibid., 123. In a similar vein, Daphne Holden and Douglas Schrock, "Performing Authentic Selfhood in an Intentional Community," in *Authenticity in Culture, Self, and Society,* ed. Vannini and Williams (Farnham, England: Ashgate, 2009), 203–17, study ways in which authenticity is performed by members of an intentional community by demonstrating spontaneity and displaying emotions. Through a life history analysis, Silviya Svejenova, "'The Path with the Heart:' Creating the Authentic Career," *Journal of Management Studies* 42, no. 5 (2005): 947–74, shows how creative individuals fashion their careers through different forms of authenticity work that involve identity expression and image manufacturing. These researchers provide examples of the everyday construction of authenticity.

10. Exemplified in the work of Peter Fleming, *Authenticity and the Cultural Politics of Work: New Forms of Informal Control* (Oxford: Oxford University Press, 2009).

11. Exemplified in the work of Shaun Naomi Tanaka, "Consuming the 'Oriental Other,' Constructing the Cosmopolitan Canadian: Reinterpreting Japanese Culinary Culture in Toronto's Japanese Restaurants" (doctoral dissertation, Queen's University, 2008). Available from ProQuest Dissertations and Theses database.

12. James H. Gilmore and B. Joseph Pine II, *Authenticity: What Consumers Really Want* (Boston: Harvard Business School Press, 2007), 3.

13. Ibid., 13.

14. Peter Fleming, *Authenticity and the Cultural Politics of Work: New Forms of Informal Control* (Oxford: Oxford University Press, 2009), 5.

15. Brian Spooner, "Weavers and Dealers: The Authenticity of an Oriental Carpet," in *The Social Life of Things: Commodities in Cultural Perspective,* ed. Arjun Appadurai (Cambridge: Cambridge University Press, 1986).

16. Tanaka, "Consuming the 'Oriental Other,'" 50.

17. Jessica M. Vasquez and Christopher Wetzel, "Tradition and the Invention of Racial Selves: Symbolic Boundaries, Collective Authenticity, and Contemporary Struggles for Racial Equality," *Ethnic and Racial Studies* 32, no. 9 (2009): 1557–75, 1557.

18. Fleming, *Authenticity and the Cultural Politics of Work*, 5.

19. The withdrawal of states from the enforcement of labor protections epitomizes a contemporary manifestation of neoliberalism. David Theo Goldberg, *The Threat of Race: Reflections on Racial Neoliberalism* (Malden, MA: Wiley-Blackwell, 2009), defines *neoliberalism* as a "shift from the caretaker or pastoral state of welfare capitalism to the 'traffic cop' or 'minimal' state, ordering flows of capital, people, goods, public services, and information" (339). In line with this, Indian local labor laws are frequently evaded, and transnational corporations or Indian subcontractors suffer few repercussions. As Henry A. Giroux, "Spectacles of Race and Pedagogies of Denial: Anti-Black Racist Pedagogy under the Reign of Neo-Liberalism," *Communication Education* 52, no. 3–4 (2003): 191–211, observes, "[U]nder neoliberal globalization, capital removes itself from any viable form of state regulation, power is uncoupled from matters of ethics and social responsibility, and market freedoms replace long-standing social contracts that once provided a safety net for the poor, the elderly, workers, and the middle class" (195).

20. "Talent Crunch, Soaring Attrition Might Push India behind Other BPO Giants: Study," *The Economic Times*, April 15, 2011, http://economictimes.indiatimes.com/tech/ites/talent-crunch-soaring-attrition-might-push-india-behind-other-bpo-giants-study/articleshow/7979564.cms (accessed July 24, 2011).

21. Baishali Kakati, "Emergence of IT & ITES—Effects on the Labour Laws," *Articlesbase*, Sept. 14, 2009, http://www.articlesbase.com/law-articles/emergence-of-it-ites-effects-on-the-labour-laws-1231331.html (accessed September 1, 2010).

22. Described as the "worst recession in a generation," in the United States there were significant job losses, housing busts, and stock market crashes. David Leonhardt, "Job Losses Show Breadth of Recession," *New York Times*, March 3, 2009, http://www.nytimes.com/2009/03/04/business/04leonhardt.html (accessed August 29, 2010).

23. These comments echo many reported on the Web site of India's BPO Union (http://bpounion.wordpress.com/category/grievancework/) and reported by other researchers such as Phil Taylor and Peter Bain, "Work Organisation and Employee Relations in Indian Call Centres," in *Developments in the Call Centre Industry: Analysis, Changes and Challenges*, ed. John Burgess and Julia Connell (London: Routledge, 2006), 36–57; Ernesto Noronha and Premilla D'Cruz, "Engaging the Professional: Organising Call Centre Agents in India," *Industrial Relations Journal* 40, no. 3 (2009): 215–34. Shehzad Nadeem, *Dead Ringers: How Outsourcing Is Changing the Way Indians Understand Themselves* (Princeton, NJ: Princeton University Press, 2011) recounts an incident where a female employee launched a complaint about a manager who offered to schedule an off day for her so he could take her to a guest house. No disciplinary action was taken, and she felt she had little choice but to resign.

24. For the history of union organizing in the sector, see Al James and Bhaskar Vira, "'Unionising' the New Spaces of the New Economy? Alternative Labour Organizing in India's IT Enabled Services—Business Process Outsourcing Industry," *Geoforum* 41, no. 3 (2010): 364–76; Ernesto Noronha and Premilla D'Cruz, "Engaging the Professional: Organising Call Centre Agents in India"; Santanu Sarkar, "Trade Unionism in Indian BPO-ITES Industry: Insights from Literature," *Indian Journal of Industrial Relations* 44, no. 1 (2008): 72–88.

25. Phil Taylor and Peter Bain, "Work Organisation and Employee Relations in Indian Call Centres."

26. Baishali Kakati, "Emergence of IT & ITES—Effects on the Labour Laws."

27. Joel S. Kahn, "Preface, Alien Worlds: Representing Cultural Otherness & A World System of Culture?" in *Culture, Multiculture, Postculture*, ed. Joel S. Kahn (London: Sage Publications, 1995).

Index

Note: *Italicized* page numbers refer to photographs.